# OFF COURSE

# OFF COURSE

✦

## Restoring Balance between Canadian Society and the Environment

*Duncan M. Taylor*

INTERNATIONAL DEVELOPMENT RESEARCH CENTRE
Ottawa • Cairo • Dakar • Johannesburg • Montevideo • Nairobi
New Delhi • Singapore

Published by the International Development Research Centre
PO Box 8500, Ottawa, ON, Canada K1G 3H9

© International Development Research Centre 1994

Taylor, D.M.

Off course : restoring balance between Canadian society and the
environment. Ottawa, ON, IDRC, 1994. ix + 139 p. : ill.

/Development strategy/, /extensive growth/, /resources exploitation/,
/sustainable development/, /environmental management/, /resources
utilization/, /industrial society/, /Canada/ — /agricultural sector/, /forestry
development/, /environmental policy/, /economic policy/, references.

UDC: 339.5:577.4(71)                              ISBN 0-88936-710-8

A microfiche edition is available.

IDRC Books endeavours to produce environmentally friendly publications.
All paper used is recycled as well as recycleable. All inks and coatings are
vegetable-based products.

# Contents

# Preface

The concept of "progress" has long intrigued men and women as they assess both themselves and the societies in which they live. The concept has often been linked with the quest for, and attainment of, a more just and equitable world, one in which pain and hardship are reduced, while health, educational, and living standards steadily improve. This "good life" has sometimes been portrayed in the form of ideal societies, or utopias, by such thinkers as Plato, Thomas More, and Francis Bacon.

With the scientific and industrial revolutions of the recent past, societies with advanced technologies could markedly improve their living standards. Understandably, "progress" became increasingly equated with the possession of more goods to consume and more services to enjoy. Moreover, these industrial societies continued to prosper and raise their consumption patterns in large part because they had access to the resources of the rest of the world, which remained in poverty. Hence, in this broad division of the world's peoples, the rich got richer and the poor got children, "and never the twain shall meet" — except on master–servant terms.

But the old order has profoundly — and irretrievably — changed in our century. Writers no longer offer us utopias but dystopias — such as Huxley's *Brave New World* and Orwell's *1984*. There is a curse attributed to the Chinese: "May you live in interesting times." And indeed we do. The rich industrial countries of the North have been matching the human poverty of their Southern counterparts by impoverishing and degrading their own environments by living in profligate fashion beyond their resource endowment. What has now become an environmental crisis — and scandal — is of global dimensions.

It is this *mutual vulnerability* of North and South — whose respective problems and challenges have in our century converged to envelop the globe — that prompted the International Development Research Centre (IDRC) to embark upon a new major project. Whereas several studies have focused on the impact on Canada of the dynamics of change in countries of the South, this book takes a different but related approach. Its purpose is to examine how a highly developed country of the North has become progressively vulnerable in a global acceleration of societal interaction and mutual transformation.

However, this study has no intention of settling for a "gloom and doom" prognosis. Throughout, its purpose is to look for viable alternatives to our planet's critical situation — in other words, how to make a 180-degree shift in South–North relations from mutual vulnerability to mutual sustainability. For Canada, what does it mean realistically to sustain and enhance both the environment and society? How can we restore the balance between Canadian society and the environment? This book offers some ideas.

*Duncan M. Taylor*
Victoria, BC, Canada
November 1994

# Acknowledgments

Participation in this project has been stimulating and calls for the pleasant acknowledgment of my indebtedness to others. It begins with Ivan Head, former President of IDRC, who initiated the concept of the project, and Paz Buttedahl, who was responsible for keeping this collaborative exercise on track. My debt of appreciation extends in turn to the Centre's highly capable editorial staff, and especially to Bill Carman.

I would also like to express my thanks to Theodora Carrol-Foster, who meticulously read the draft manuscript and offered insightful criticisms coupled with suggestions designed to strengthen and enhance the overall thrust of the thesis. I appreciate too the permission given by Robert Gibson, editor of *Alternatives: Perspectives on Society, Technology and Environment,* to make use of materials previously published in his journal on the genesis of expansionist and ecological world views.

The section on forestry in British Columbia has had the benefit of constructive input and feedback from Jeremy Wilson of the University of Victoria's Department of Political Science. In turn, thanks go out to Paul Senez and Lesley Hall for data on Canadian agriculture. And last, but far from least, I thank Tracey Tanaka for all those creative hours she spent working on the manuscript and the graphics.

*Chapter 1*

# The Need for
# Remedial Action

*Over and above the moral contract with God, over and above the social contract concluded with men, we must now conclude an ethical and political contract with nature, with this Earth to which we owe our very existence and which gives us life. To the ancients...nature was the abode of the divinities that gave the forest, the desert, or the mountains a personality which commanded worship and respect. The Earth had a soul. To find that soul again, to give it new life, that is the essence of Rio.*

— Boutros Boutros-Ghali

The developing countries of the South are being exposed increasingly to the consequences of an interconnected set of problems: environmental, economic, social, and political. However, the industrially and technologically advanced countries of the North are becoming progressively vulnerable to these same problems, sometimes with different consequences. This book discusses the worsening environmental and societal nexus in Canada, one of the most advanced technological and economic countries of the North, and a member of the Group of Seven (G-7).

The book was completed after the Rio Earth Summit of 1992, whose agenda, successes, and failed opportunities alike provide a vivid overview of the parlous state of our planetary environment. What is becoming more apparent daily is that the countries of the North and South have become mutually vulnerable to global developments. They are in a free-fall toward what could be a cataclysmic outcome in the next century unless drastic remedial action is initiated on a global scale — action in which Canada must obviously be involved.

It is that "mutual vulnerability" which is at the core of this study. In his recent work, *On a Hinge of History*, Ivan Head points to "the extraordinary imbalance that has developed between North and South" (Head 1991, pp. 20–21). Here he is using a form of shorthand to distinguish between the world's industrial countries, which constitute the "North," and the developing societies of the "South." This distinction can also be expressed in rough geographical terms (Roche 1993, p. 77):

> *There is a line running around the world from the Mexico–US border through the Mediterranean, over Afghanistan, Mongolia and China and down below Japan into the Pacific Ocean. This is the fundamental division of North and South. North of the line, the population is a little over a billion; south of the line, it is over 4 billion.*

According to Head, although the most obvious consequences of this growing imbalance are environmental degradation, economic uncertainty, social unrest, and political instability, underlying these problems is a major ethical challenge that must be addressed. The global issues we are confronted with are not merely managerial and technological problems. Perhaps more than anything else, they point to a profound cultural crisis — a crisis in our current values and ways of thinking.

This crisis has been precipitated for a number of reasons. For instance, unprecedented and exponential growth has occurred in contemporary times in our physical and societal environments, resulting in the following:

✦   A fourfold population increase in the 20th century;

✦   Creation of a global economy, but one marked by increasing disparities between rich and poor regions;

✦   Accelerating depletion of the planet's resources, with degradation of its ecosystems upon which all species, including humans, depend for survival; and

✦   A concomitant increase of pollution and environmental destruction on every continent.

In this century, the global economy has expanded 20 times, the consumption of fossil fuels has grown by a factor of 30, and the industrial production has increased by a factor of 50 — most of this growth taking place since 1950 (MacNeill 1990, p. 1). These growth curves cannot continue indefinitely for at least two reasons:

◆ The planet has limited resources.

◆ The planet's viability as an ecological system may already be approaching an irreversible breakdown.

These international disequilibriums are challenging us to go beyond our narrow nationalisms and to extend our moral boundaries in ever-widening circles to include other peoples, species, and life-forms. These disequilibriums also give us an opportunity to acquire a deeper empathy for other cultures and regions and, with it, a qualitative shift in emphasis frcm our traditional boundaried sense of independence to acceptance of ecological and societal interdependence. In short, we are increasingly faced with the limitations and inadequacies of our current dominant world view and the pressing need to adopt a very different set of values and assumptions; ones that are more in keeping with evolving societal and ecological imperatives.

For instance, environmental degradation is currently challenging the very roots of modernity, based as it is on the North's growth ethos. The industrialized North has historically committed itself to this growth ethos on the assumption that the planet's resources were all but limitless, to be exploited maximally and with impunity. Moreover, the North had the "right" to carry this resource exploitation into the South as it saw fit — in other words, wherever profitable.

Here it is important to point out that Northern countries no longer have a monopoly on this kind of behaviour. Parts of the South are currently engaged in unprecedented economic activity. Indeed, the Asian side of the Pacific Rim is witnessing the world's greatest economic growth. This spectacular transformation — which in the next century could call for a redrawing of the current North–South demarcation boundary — is led by what the popular media call the "dragons and tigers." The southern part of China qualifies as a "dragon" of potentially vast dimensions; Hong Kong, Singapore,

South Korea, and Taiwan prove their mettle as "tigers" daily. In addition, Indonesia, Malaysia, and Thailand are working hard to gain membership in this new "North-within-the-South" economic fraternity. This phenomenon is largely financed and controlled by the North's corporate elite using the latest imported technologies. In turn, it is directed by a well-educated managerial class imbued with the North's growth ethos, value system, and behavioural and consumption patterns.

However, the "myth of superabundance" is fast becoming ecologically untenable. And so Northern nations, and their North-within-the-South counterparts, will have to give way progressively to a new set of values for tomorrow's world — values that integrate redefined concepts of development with overriding environmental sustainability. In turn, Canada cannot hope to insulate itself from these problems because it is both an integral part of the planetary ecology and an integral part of the larger human community.

This crucial concept of "sustainability" brings us directly to the thesis and overriding thrust of the Brundtland Report, *Our Common Future,* by the World Commission on Environment and Development (WCED 1987). Yet, the concepts "sustainability" and "development," with chameleonic adaptability, have come to mean many things to many people. All too often, the term "sustainable development" is used to reinforce some of the worst aspects of an expansionist world view, which in its current form is unsustainable.

This book takes on the following approach:

✦ An historical overview of the North's — and therefore Canada's — commitment to the expansionist ethos;

✦ An examination of the way in which the term "sustainable development" is being used to support both a dominant expansionist world view and an emerging ecological world view;

✦ A critique of Canada's commitment to the expansionist position (the crisis facing Canada's two largest resource sectors — forestry and agriculture — are given as examples of the need to rethink contemporary economic and environmental policies); and, finally,

✦ Recommendations for a strategy of resource usage that is based on a systemic approach to Canada's social, economic, and biophysical domains and that is committed to comprehensive environmental sustainability.

In turn, by examining these areas, specific issues will also be addressed regarding Canada's international environmental responsibility and the need to shift the South–North relationship from its current state of mutual vulnerability toward one of mutual sustainability.

# Chapter 2

# Canada in a Global Context

*T*he Earth is one but the world is not. We all depend on one *biosphere for sustaining our lives. Yet each community, each country, strives for survival and prosperity with little regard for its impact on others. Some consume the Earth's resources at a rate that would leave little for future generations. Others, many more in number, consume far too little and live with the prospect of hunger, squalor, disease, and early death.*
— *Our Common Future* (WCED 1987)

Many of the development paths followed by industrialized countries of the North are not viable. The folly of continuing in these ways should be of concern to governments in the South, especially if they wish to avoid falling into the trap of accepting without question the worst models exported from the North. Policymakers in both the North and the South should now combine their efforts to counteract the planet's burgeoning human population and deteriorating physical environment. In short, all of us must immediately embark on a course of development that is sustainable.

However, the economies of the South will have to continue to grow to redress some of the wretched disparities between South and North and to offset the erosion of economic gain as a result of the rapid increase in world population. If this growth is to occur without causing irreversible damage to the planet's ecology, the North must dramatically cut back on its current level of consumption.

But there is an emerging issue of increasing importance in Southern societies. This is the issue of accelerating and unregulated growth in consumption attitudes, demands, and growth in the South, especially among the expanding middle and upper classes. For example, India has a middle and upper class of over 250 million, with the same consumer appetites as their Northern counterparts. Unfortunately, as attested by the results of the 1992 Rio Earth Summit, we have yet to come to grips with the radical political and economic changes that will be required to move Canada and other nations in this direction of reduced consumption. Moreover, couching the argument in simple North–South terms tends to obfuscate some equally destructive trends occurring within countries as well as between regions in the South.

Finding practical solutions to putting humanity on the path to sustainable development was to have been the goal of the Rio Earth Summit. Twenty years earlier, at the Stockholm Conference, it was acknowledged that the entrenched nature of the nation-state system remained a major stumbling block to global action. And yet the *Rio Declaration on Environment and Development* refused to budge on this issue when it declared that states should have "the sovereign right to exploit their own resources" (UNCED 1992, Principle 2).

The disappointment of not coming to terms with a number of these major issues was reflected by Maurice Strong, the Canadian secretary-general of the Rio Earth Summit, when, in his closing remarks (Rusk and Vincent 1992, p. A10), he alluded to the failure of the Stockholm Conference: "The only difference is that now we don't have another twenty years to squander." Leaders of nations from both the South and the North still proclaimed the virtues of economic growth. Perhaps it is significant that a conference of the G-7 leaders was held in Munich less than a month later — there, the focus of concern was economic growth, not environmental sustainability. However, as Norwegian Prime Minister Gro Harlem Brundtland (Rusk and Vincent 1992, p. A1) warned the Rio delegates:

> *There is no turning back from realizing that we are heading toward a crisis of uncontrollable dimensions unless we change course. The north as well as the rich in the south will have to change consumption and production patterns.*

Jim MacNeill, who, along with Maurice Strong, made a significant contribution to the 1987 Brundtland Report (*Our Common Future*), has suggested that a major failure of the Rio Earth Summit was to isolate the concepts of "sustainable" and "development." This polarized the debate and made environmental protection and economic development mutually exclusive (Rusk and Vincent 1992, p. A10). Not surprisingly, the split was along traditional South–North lines: the countries of the South arguing for massive economic development, and the countries of the North arguing for more environmental protection, within a dominant economic growth model.

Since *Our Common Future*, the term "sustainable development" has been adopted by groups espousing conflicting interests and values. These groups range from environmental "preservationists" and "deep ecologists" to advocates of intensified resource development, and from those who argue for increased state intervention to those who are apologists for neoconservatism and the recent international trend toward market-driven economics. The adaptability of the term is remarkable.

Beneath this confusion lies a conflict between fundamentally antithetical world views (Capra 1986). Each view has its own set of assumptions about knowledge and values, including its own vision of the proper human–environment relationship. These two extreme views may be referred to, respectively, as the "expansionist world view" and the "ecological world view" — the former being the dominant model and the latter still emerging and not yet fully developed. In this book, each will be defined to help clarify the term "sustainable development" and how it is currently being used in both national and international forums.

## How Did We Get into This Predicament?

Since the beginning of the Industrial Revolution, the world's population and industrialization have increased exponentially, as have the levels of global pollution and environmental degradation. In turn, planetary life-support systems and resources required to sustain this demographic and economic growth are decreasing at an alarming rate. Humanity has been described as the "agent and victim of global change," which raises a critical question:

◆ Can we sustain indefinite development — especially economic development — at our current rate of societal growth and resource usage, and do so within an environment that must itself remain sustainable if humanity — and with it the planet — is to survive?

Historically, there have been three demographic "surges." The first was in Palaeolithic times (Old Stone Age, pre-8000 BC); the second began with Neolithic agriculture (around 8000 BC); and the third, in modern times. The total world population before Neolithic agriculture was estimated at 5 million. Currently, the world's population is about 5.6 billion. It is projected to reach 6.2 billion by the year 2000 and at least 10 billion by 2050 (Figure 1).

A doubling time of 1 500 years brought global numbers to about 500 million in 1650 AD. A reduction of the doubling time to 200 years raised the population to 1 billion by 1850. It then took only 80 years for this figure to double to 2 billion and 40 more years to double

**World population (billions)**

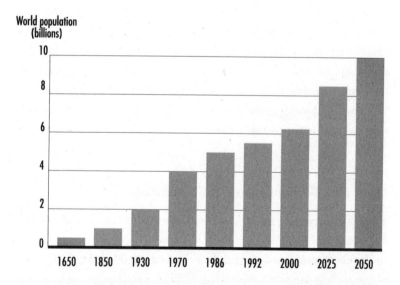

Figure 1. Global population growth: 1650 to 2050 (source: World Bank 1991).

again to 4 billion in 1970. In the late 1990s, the annual net increase in the number of people will average close to 92 million — or some three times the population of Canada. In the coming century, the world population will continue to grow, but at a somewhat slower rate. Projections call for 8.4 billion as of 2025 and 10 billion by 2050. Yet, by the end of the next century, the world could contain 11.3 billion people, with 1.3 billion in the North, and 10 billion in the South (World Bank 1991, pp. xvii–xx).

These population surges have been accompanied by increased control, through technological advances, of the three layers of the Earth's surface: land (lithosphere), water (hydrosphere), and air (atmosphere). At the same time, the speed at which these changes have occurred has also increased. This evolutionary dynamic has been massive because it reversed our species' original relationship to its planetary habitat.

As with other species, ours originally evolved in a state of relative symbiotic adaptation to the environment, but with at least one major difference: our tool-making capability and our increasing capacity to alter the natural environment. This capability has been responsible for the shift to an accelerating exploitation of our physical environment. Our Palaeolithic ancestors were so few and possessed such relatively simple tools that for scores of millennia they did little more than live off the interest of the global environmental capital. In terms of systems theory, just as the evolution of the geosphere and biosphere has been dominated by self-maintenance — or negative-feedback — processes, so Stone Age societies were dominated by behaviour patterns that emphasized maintaining an overall balance with their environment.

Our socioeconomic and technological systems, devised in recent centuries and driven by positive-feedback processes — hence, the "growth" dynamic — have been increasingly diminishing the planet's endowment of inorganic and organic capital. This behaviour is justified within an expansionist world view that regards material growth as indispensable to our "pursuit of happiness." Its absence, we are warned, can only result in loss of incentive, stagnation, and mass unemployment. Such a paradigm of continuous growth

(measured quantitatively by a society's gross national product or
GNP) assumes that there will always be an unfailing supply of
resources — an assumption rejected by many ecologists as the "myth
of superabundance."

## Is "Sustainable Development" Sustainable?

In 1983, the United Nations General Assembly established the World
Commission on Environment and Development with a mandate to
formulate "a global agenda for change" and to propose "long-term
environmental strategies for achieving sustainable development by
the year 2000 and beyond" (WCED 1987, p. ix). Perhaps the most
positive contribution of its final report, *Our Common Future* (WCED
1987), was to marry ecology and economy on a global scale, and to
focus on the critical problems resulting from that relationship. The
report has emphasized that "ecological exhaustion will increasingly
feed back on the economy to cripple production without significant
change in economic practice" (Clow 1990, p. 6). With continued
irrefutable logic, it links the environment–development nexus to the
crisis of endemic poverty in the South.

However, it fails to define what is expected from the geosphere's
and biosphere's resource endowment to meet the increased economic activity envisaged for expanded development in the South,
as well as the expected growth in the North. What assurance have
we that the biosphere can indefinitely cope with the ecological side
effects of increased economic activities with the resultant wastes and
mounting toxic materials? Already, the alarming loss of atmospheric
ozone as a result of widespread use of chlorofluorocarbons (CFCs)
has caused scientists concern about the long-term effect of increased
solar radiation on terrestrial and aquatic plant photosynthesis. A
change in photosynthesis would have an impact on marine phyto-
plankton and its ability to reproduce itself and thereby remain the
major source of planetary oxygen, an essential aquatic food source,
and a major sink for carbon dioxide.

*Our Common Future* also relies on managing resources to obtain
"maximum sustainable yield," although there could be great risks in

attempting to obtain "maximum" rather than "optimum" sustainable yield. Apart from the difficulties of quantifying "maximum" sustainability, past experience shows that such yields are unreasonable. According to Clow (1990, p. 7):

> [They] are so bent by wishful thinking, corporate pressures and ignorance that they are usually many times too high. The example of Atlantic Canada's fish stock estimates and catch quotas is tangible proof of this point.

In 1994, we have seen the possible permanent collapse of the Atlantic fishery — which was hitherto a renewable resource.

At the heart of *Our Common Future* is the thesis that global society must achieve "sustainable development" that "meets the needs of the present without compromising the ability of future generations to meet their own needs" (WCED 1987, p. 43). But what happens if each succeeding generation expects to consume, as its right, as much or even more than the previous generation? "Sustainable development" has become a "motherhood" term. Who can be against it? It may be argued that "sustainable development" is an oxymoron in terms of the values of our dominant world view and current economic assumptions. Put simply, although our economies are predicated on the need for continual growth, the ecosystems within which they are embedded are not. Consequently, as William Rees (1990a, p. 9) argues, the "consumption of ecological resources everywhere has begun to exceed sustainable rates of biological production." In Canada, as we shall see, one highly visible example is found in cutting down the forests of British Columbia, well in excess of long-term sustainable yield levels.

The underlying imperatives of growth-oriented economies are at loggerheads with the realities of ecological systems. This is illustrated dramatically by net primary production (NPP), which is the rate at which plants produce usable food or chemical energy. It is estimated that up to 40 percent of terrestrial NPP (from photosynthesis) has already been used up by humans modifying and destroying planetary ecosystems. Given the fact that *Homo sapiens* is but one of millions of species, a doubling of the human population together with a 5- to 10-fold increase in economic activity would leave no more NPP for other species — without which humans cannot survive (Vitousek et al. 1986, pp. 368–374).

Ecologists warn that we cannot continue our appropriation of NPP; *Our Common Future*, however, adopts a different approach (p. 213):

> *Given expected population growth, a five- to tenfold increase in world industrial output can be anticipated by the time world population stabilizes sometime in the next century.*

What are the implications of this in the energy field, on which future development must depend? Already no energy sources meet the criteria of dependability, safety, and environmental soundness. Using the terawatt-year (TWY) as an energy unit equivalent to approximately 1 billion tonnes of coal, the report estimates that global energy consumption amounted to some 10 TWY in 1980. If per-capita use were to remain at this same level, by 2025 a global population of 8.4 billion would need almost 14 TWY (over 4 TWY in developing countries and over 9 TWY in industrialized countries), an increase of 40 percent from 1980 levels. From *Our Common Future* (WCED 1987, pp. 169–170):

> *If energy consumption per head became uniform world-wide at current industrial country levels, by 2025 that same global population would require about 55 [TWY].*

What can we deduce from these figures?

✦ First, to keep the global energy consumption increase to 40 percent, the current disparity in North–South economic standards must be maintained.

✦ Second, if the South is to attain economic parity with the North, global energy consumption must increase 5½ times.

✦ Third, as of 2025, the global population will still be decades away from reaching a steady state because of the sheer unstoppable momentum of population growth (sometimes referred to as "demographic inertia") after birthrates have fallen.

As the report points out, however, neither the "low" nor the "high" energy requirement will likely prove realistic; a "generally acceptable pathway to a safe and sustainable energy future has not yet been found" (WCED 1987, p. 169).

What else does this anticipated 5- to 10-fold increase in global economic activity suggest? When the report was released in 1987, this activity had reached $13 trillion (US), with most of it controlled by about one-fifth of the world's population. Just to enable the South to reach the North's current resource usage and GNP would call for a fivefold increase to a global economic activity of some $65 trillion. But if the North doubles its own growth in the meantime — a modest increase considering that industrial production "has grown more than fiftyfold over the past century," with four-fifths of this growth since 1950 (WCED 1987, p. 4) — we arrive at the 10-fold increase hypothesized in the report, bringing global economic activity to $130 trillion. Either figure must dramatically exacerbate the current environmental crisis: 5-fold or 10-fold is beyond the planet's carrying capacity.

Some years ago, we encountered the term "demographic inertia" to indicate the momentum of the current population explosion. Demographic inertia is analogous to a supertanker moving with a full cargo. Even after its engines are shut down, the tanker will still travel many kilometres before coming to a halt, unless the engines are reversed to increase the slowdown. Given the "head of steam" of industrial economies and technologies, what will it take to overcome the thrust of "societal inertia" to achieve sustainable development? Will the engines of economic and demographic growth have to be reversed to save the environment?

At the Stockholm Conference in 1972, and again, though to a lesser extent, at the 1992 Earth Summit in Rio, many countries from the South, backed by the Vatican, rejected the limits-to-growth thesis as a highly sophisticated form of neocolonialism. They were prepared to accept environmental pollution — the rich countries' disease — to industrialize and improve their living standards. In calling for a markedly substantial increase in the South's development, the Brundtland Report neglects to raise the related question:

✦ To what extent must the North cut back on its own rate of resource consumption to make this growth possible?

## From Mutual Vulnerability
## to Mutual Sustainability

The Brundtland Report has forcefully argued that growth must be undertaken in the South to meet fundamental needs relating to basic survival and quality of life, to achieve social equity and self-determination, and to maintain ecological integrity (Gardner and Roseland 1989, pp. 36–48). It is becoming increasingly apparent that these major transformations can only be achieved by a critical strategy. In short, the North, where the largest amount of the 40-fold increase in industrial production since 1950 has occurred, must lessen its monopoly on global resources and cut consumption drastically so that the South can survive.

Currently, 26 percent of the world's population consumes 80 to 86 percent of the planet's nonrenewable resources and 34 to 53 percent of global food products (WCED 1987, p. 33). By the middle of the next century, the North's population may well be only 10 percent of the global population. Can the North still expect to continue its current consumption ratio? How realistic is it to expect that the South, with 90 percent of the population by 2050, will accept its minuscule proportion of global resources?

The report has noted the close links between material poverty, social inequity, and the degradation of the environment. Moreover, three-quarters of the world's flora and fauna lies between latitudes 20° North and 20° South, where there is the greatest need for an enormous investment in environmental restoration and protection of specific terrestrial and aquatic areas. Consequently, if only for our own long-term sustainability and enlightened self-interest, let alone for the very survival of the South, the North must transfer large quantities of its material, financial, and technological resources.

This will call for some ingenious rethinking of economic theory. Increasingly, we will be faced with the dilemma that the very growth that currently impoverishes our environment may well be needed to generate the vast sums of money that will be required to achieve national and international environmental restoration. Moreover, Canada's federal debt by early 1994 was already half a trillion dollars and steadily rising, and, in an era of increasing economic hardship and fiscal restraint, Canadians may be less willing and able to put their finances toward national and international social and environmental concerns.

There is no question that the South will develop. For our mutual survival, it must develop. The question facing all of us is along what lines will this development occur? This is the bargaining chip of the nations of the South. Unless Canada and other privileged nations of the North dramatically cut back on their consumption of energy and resources, and the resultant wastes produced, .they can hardly demand environmentally sustainable forms of development from countries in the South.

Development strategies that are environmentally as well as socially sustainable challenge the concept of "development" the North has promulgated through the expansionist world view. Historically, technological and developmental strategies have often failed to take into account the needs of specific cultures and the long-term effects on ecological systems. Too frequently, "development" has become "maldevelopment" when inappropriate programs from the North are improperly implemented by Southern governments (Shiva 1989, pp. 14–37). This has destroyed cultural and spiritual values of indigenous peoples, and left them without the knowledge and skills needed to protect and restore specific ecosystems. These criticisms are as valid for development projects in northern Canada as for Amazonia and Borneo.

Judging a culture or society to be "underdeveloped" implies that there is only one acceptable route for societal evolution — that of the North's industrialized countries. Consequently, "developing" regions are labeled as inferior until they achieve some measure of scientific and technological parity with the North. To define "development" in terms of the North's industrialization is to subscribe uncritically to an expansionist world view with the attendant strategies that are currently creating havoc with much of the planet's self-balancing processes.

## The Environmental Crisis
## Reflects a Cultural Crisis

Although the Brundtland Report stresses the need to integrate economic policies with environmental requirements, Canadian federal and provincial governments have been accused (especially by environmental groups) of doing little more than paying lip service to this concept. For example, the provincial roundtables, which were established to formulate sustainable development strategies, have been criticized for the way in which their members were recruited, as well as their tendency to give preferential treatment to special interest groups — especially business (Howlett 1990, pp. 580-601). And to the extent that these roundtables have made progress, they tend to face ongoing government inertia and private sector antagonism. Indeed, "sustainable development," for the most part, continues to be interpreted by Canada's federal and provincial governments in terms of the values of the expansionist world view and is in danger of perpetuating many of the worst aspects of the status quo. Indeed, our politicians' lack of real concern about environmental sustainability was all too apparent during the federal election of 1993 when the need to link the ongoing health of the economy to the ongoing health of the environment was regarded as a nonissue.

In preparing for a sustainable society, we must be clear about one thing — the status quo will not suffice. Perhaps more than at any other time in history, Canadians are faced with a series of crises — constitutional and political, economic and environmental — all of which are undermining the relevance of traditional policies and institutions. Moreover, as Canada's long-term societal and environmental sustainability is inextricably linked to the welfare of the rest of the planet, any discussions regarding sustainable development must be predicated upon a restructured South–North dialogue. If global economic output cannot grow an estimated 5 to 10 times without irreversible damage to the planetary ecology, then the North will have to reduce its use of resources so that the South may live. Undoubtedly, this will require a profound and dramatic shift in our current political and economic policies and thinking. In turn, we must acknowledge that the current crisis is more than an environmental one. It involves a complete rethinking of the relevance and validity of much of contemporary Western culture as well as the tenets and beliefs of an expansionist world view.

# Chapter 3

# Canada's Vulnerability

*E*ach *man is locked into a system that compels him to increase his herd without limit — in a world that is limited. Ruin is the destination toward which all men rush, each pursuing his own best interest in a society that believes in the freedom of the commons. Freedom in a commons brings ruin to all.*

— Hardin (1977, p. 20)

## The Expansionist World View: Sustaining Development

For more than two decades, the "tragedy of the commons" has been a powerful theme and rallying cry for environmentalists around the world. Popularized by biologist Garrett Hardin in the late 1960s, its force lies less in its literal historical accuracy than in its analogy to the plight of modern society. The "tragedy" points to the consequences that inevitably result from the unrestrained exploitation of a finite environment by individuals or nation-states acting for their own immediate self-interest. For Hardin, the three following conditions must be present for the tragedy of the commons to occur:

✦ The commons or resources must be finite;

✦ There must be a consumption pattern that removes more than it puts back in; and

✦ The users of the commons must be motivated by selfishness, rather than by enlightened self- and public interest.

The recent collapse of the Canadian northern cod stock, with the resultant loss of approximately 40 thousand jobs in Newfoundland's fishing industry, in many ways exemplifies this theme.

For the past 450 years, the Western world has managed to avoid many of the problems associated with scarcity. With the discovery of the New World and with the increasing ability of technology to exploit the natural environment, we have witnessed an unprecedented era of seeming abundance. Many of the values underlying Western industrial society, such as the belief in liberal democracy, laissez-faire capitalism, freedom, and individualism, were predicated historically on the assumption of resource abundance (Ophuls 1977, pp. 143–145). Consequently, 17th and 18th century political and economic theorists, such as John Locke (1632–1704) and Adam Smith (1723–1790), looked forward to an era of material wealth and an end to the authoritarian political institutions that had hitherto characterized an age of resource scarcity.

Similarly, in his famous frontier thesis written during the 1890s, Frederick Jackson Turner saw free western land in the United States as an explanation for American individualism and democracy. Walter Prescott Webb extended this thesis to include both sides of the Atlantic, so that overseas exploration created a "Great Frontier," at once geographical, political, economic, and cultural, which assured the West hegemony over the rest of the world. Europe's area of control expanded from its own continental 8.6 million square kilometres to approximately 52 million square kilometres of control over other continents — Africa, Asia, Australia, and North and South America — and ushered in a boom period lasting from 1500 to 1914. During that time, commercial and industrial revolutions were accompanied by the creation of colonial empires, access to overseas raw materials, and the establishment of a global market. This boom period was marked by unprecedented growth, with Western nation-states extending their dominion by military, political, and economic means.

In light of Webb's thesis, we can ask: What happens after the Great Frontier has been explored and the boom period is over? How will our Western institutions, fashioned and formalized in an era of unprecedented geographical growth, adjust to the end of *terra incognita?*

On the one hand, the political theorist William Ophuls has suggested that our current liberal values are grossly maladapted to an era of increasing resource scarcity. To protect the environmental commons, Ophuls (1977, pp. 147–165) fears that rampant individualism will be replaced by a form of communalism, and that liberalism, in turn, will have to give way to authoritarian political institutions capable of enforcing the needs of a steady-state and conserver society.

On the other hand, is it reasonable to place our faith in the "technological fix" to maintain a state of resource abundance? Certainly this is the hope of a great many people. Recently, the announced discovery of "cold fusion" gave hope of unlimited energy, only to be proved highly premature. Meanwhile, the war with Iraq helped to underscore how extremely vulnerable our industrial society is to a potential decline in the availability of fossil fuels. Advocates of the "technological fix" have suggested that it is only a matter of time before we are capable of exploiting the resources of extraterrestrial environments. In the meantime, however, we must concern ourselves with our planet's rapidly diminishing resources and recognize that, for all intents and purposes, we have come to the end of the global frontier.

So, we have to ask ourselves this: Just how can our planet's ecosystem, with its finite boundaries and resources, support the current dual impact of industrial technology and a global population that will continue to increase for decades in the 21st century? How much longer can it act as a "sink" for absorbing our wastes and pollution? This is fast becoming a major problem over and above the exploitation of resources. As well, we have to face such problems as massive malnutrition and actual starvation in many areas of the Third World and parts of the urbanized North; soil erosion and desertification; the destruction of tropical and temperate rain forests in the Amazon Valley, Clayoquot Sound, and elsewhere; air and water pollution, including acid rain; the continuing extinction of thousands of species of flora and fauna; and science's frightening warnings about puncturing the ozone layer and the ever-mounting "greenhouse effect." In addition, we have scarcely begun to take account of our rapidly growing mountains of toxic and other waste materials and the insidious and long-term effects of the "chemicalization" of modern society on the future health and survival of the human and myriad other species.

The expansionist world view is grounded in the concept of continuous growth, extrapolated optimistically into a seemingly boundless future. Its philosophical roots are found in a variety of sources: Francis Bacon's advocacy of the inductive method to control nature for human ends; the Cartesian and Newtonian view of the universe as a "Great Machine," subject to methodologies predicated upon reductionism, quantification, and the separation of facts and values; the Enlightenment's faith in the wedding of science to technology for harnessing nature's resources to end problems of human scarcity and suffering; and the first Industrial Revolution's technological advances, which dramatically helped to equate "progress" with the satisfaction of material wants and eventually to create a consumer-oriented society.

In the expansionist world view, nature is seen essentially as a storehouse of resources to be employed for the satisfaction of ever-increasing material needs by an ever-increasing human population. Conversely, this approach all but ignores the indispensable role of the natural biophysical environment to act as a "sink" to recycle and process waste materials and maintain ecological functions. Furthermore, this perspective equates material growth with development, which, in turn, is regarded as a prerequisite for human happiness and prosperity. Moreover, its proponents claim that any drop in this growth rate must inevitably result in stagnation, mass unemployment, and distress. Rejecting the goal of a "steady-state" society (where economic activities have to be limited by the constraints imposed by physical ecosystems), its advocates argue that technological advances can be relied upon to increase global standards of living, harness renewable and more environmentally "friendly" sources of energy, and increase food production and the availability of other biological products through breakthroughs in biotechnology. More efficient technologies are expected to solve the problems created by previous technologies, to create substitutes for depleted resources, and to replace damaged environments. In short, the expansionist position rejects the implications of the doctrine of increasing natural resource scarcity (the need to drastically cut back Northern consumption and resource exploitation) on the grounds that we can rely on technology to invalidate its thesis.

Applying the logic of this position to Canadian resource policy, we should be using our resources to their fullest extent to secure benefits for the present because many of them will likely become obsolete or considerably less important in the years ahead. During the Trudeau administration, Trade Minister Jean-Luc Pepin, in defending the government's decision to sell natural gas to the United States, summed up this position (Burton 1977, p.17) when he argued:

> It would be crazy to sit on it. In maybe 25 to 50 years, we'll kick ourselves in the pants for not capitalizing on what we had when gas and oil were current commodities.

The expansionist world view arose with capitalism; but, in this century, capitalist and socialist countries alike applied the basic tenets of the expansionist position. Indeed, it remains the dominant social paradigm (Milbrath 1989, pp. 115–134). It is noteworthy that the socialists began as critics, especially of social abuses, and that many of their works included attacks on the narrow view of humans as possessive, economic individuals. Karl Marx, like Adam Smith, was a child of the Enlightenment in his devotion to technological and material progress.

A major tenet in recent times is the belief that human needs and wants can best be satisfied through ever-expanding economic growth. In a market-dominated global economy, seemingly limitless expansion is regarded as essential both to stimulate and to satisfy these needs and wants, which, because we live in a largely secular age, are deemed to be solvable in material terms. The persuasiveness of this perspective is evident in the eagerness of Eastern Europe to embrace the capitalist ethic following the collapse of state socialism. Critics of the expansionist world view, however, point out that this is much like rearranging the deck chairs on the *Titanic*. One may change the position of the chairs from left to right and from state ownership to private ownership; however, this doesn't address the central problem that the industrial ship of state is in grave jeopardy and what may be needed is a new ship.

Much of the impetus for this expansionist ethos was related historically to the West's geopolitical triumph. Although the physical frontier was progressively pushed back until, by the end of the last century, there remained few unexplored areas of human habitation, this expansionist ethos has remained an integral part of our industrial model. Today, the burden of proof is upon its exponents to show that it can effectively withstand the need for limits to growth. Hence, we are on the horns of a dilemma. We are confronted increasingly with the need to limit our growth and, at the same time, the industrial countries of the world are structured on the need for such growth to maintain their economic and social stability. At the 1992 Earth Summit in Rio, US President George Bush reaffirmed his country's commitment to the expansionist position by rejecting a call from the South for a cutback in Northern consumption. As Bush remarked (Rusk and Vincent 1992, pp. A1–A2):

> [Economic growth is] the engine of change and the friend of the environment.... We believe that the road to Rio must point toward both environmental protection and economic growth, environment and development. And by now it's clear, to sustain development, we must protect the environment; and to protect the environment, we must sustain development.

In turn, the United States went on to reject a biodiversity treaty that might limit the future range of US patents in biotechnology, although President Clinton has since reversed this decision and, further, established the President's Council on Sustainable Development. Arguing for environmental conservation within an expansionist world view model is not new, but this apparent paradox needs explanation.

## "Wise Management Conservation": Working Within the System

With the rise of the modern conservation movement at the turn of the last century, both in the United States and in Canada, conservation was soon to become an ally of the expansionist position. Indeed, the "wise use" school of Gifford Pinchot in the United States and Clifford Sifton in Canada equated conservation with "sustainable exploitation." For both Pinchot and Sifton, conservation should work against the wastefulness and environmentally disruptive excesses of a developing society, but not against development per se. They made it clear that conservation was not to be confused with preservation or allowing nature to remain in its original state. Ideally, conservation would mean that "wise scientific management" procedures were used to develop all natural resources, including forests, soils, water, and wildlife. Moreover, wherever possible, these resources would be harvested as a renewable crop so that nature's resources could be "used" and "saved" simultaneously.

Since the early years of this century, the "wise management" school has prevailed as the dominant voice of conservation in North America. In many respects, this was due to its pragmatic allegiance to the underlying economic values of this period. Until relatively recently, arguments for conservation have been almost solely on a cost–benefit basis. By placing conservation clearly on the side of economic "progress," proponents of this approach were able to achieve a level of influence unmatched by their "preservationist" counterparts.

With this history, and given the rise of neoconservative thought during the 1980s in Canada and throughout the Western world, it is understandable that the Canadian federal government's response to the Brundtland Report's call for a sustainable development strategy should be subsumed within the framework of the expansionist world view. This stance was to be reiterated at the 1992 Rio Earth Summit by a majority of countries from both the North and the South. The Canadian government's National Task Force report (Canadian Council of Resource and Environment Ministers 1987) refers to "sustainable economic development" and the need to maintain "economic growth" insofar as "economic growth and prosperity provide us with the capability to support wise resource management and protect environmental quality." It states (Canadian Council of Resource and Environment Ministers 1987, p. 3):

> *Sustainable development is the requirement that current practices should not diminish the possibility of maintaining or improving living standards in the future...sustainable development does not*

*require the preservation of the current stock of natural resources
or any mix of human, physical and natural assets. Nor does it place
artificial limits on economic growth, provided that such growth is
both economically and environmentally sustainable.*

It is not difficult to see why Canadian business leaders supported
the report. Critics of the basic characteristics of prevailing human–
environment relations were less satisfied.

For the critics, development of the current kind is not sustainable. In fact, the current expansionist paradigm lies at the root of
the global environmental crisis. But, as William Rees (1988, p. 135),
a resource ecologist at the University of British Columbia, points out:

*The Task Force is reluctant to admit the possibility that living
standards for some may have to be reduced that others may live at
all. It avoids this issue entirely.*

This sort of criticism has led to the suggestion that the term
"sustainable development" is being co-opted by established interests
and used to promote scientific and managerial devices, offering
"band-aid" solutions that mask the need for structural changes at
political and economic levels. The changes that are needed to
address national and international problems involve ecological
integrity and the basic needs of social self-determination and equity.

# Chapter 4

# How Canada Has Misused Its Environmental Endowment

*F*<sub>our</sub> *decades of a cheap food policy has wreaked havoc in agriculture, pushing it into unsustainable practices, just so I could buy bread for a dollar.*

— Gayton (1990, p. 144)

*There is a growing realization that for Canadian agriculture it can no longer be business as usual. If the industry is to compete in world markets and satisfy environmental concerns, modest accommodations will not be enough.*

— Science Council of Canada (1992)

## Agriculture in Crisis

The above statement from the Science Council of Canada is taken from a recent report which argues that the Canadian agricultural food industry is in a state of crisis. It goes on to argue that the status quo is no longer viable as there is "mounting evidence that economic sustainability is jeopardized by the neglect of the physical and biological resource on which agriculture depends" (Science Council of Canada 1992, p. 13).

Agriculture remains a cornerstone of the Canadian economy. As such, it is a $50 billion (CA) a year industry that directly and indirectly employs 14 percent of the country's work force and contributes approximately one-third of the nation's trade surplus. Yet, only 5 percent of Canada's land base has the capacity to sustain agricultural food crops and virtually all of this is currently being used, leaving little room for future expansion of food production.

Ultimately, all civilizations depend on the ecological availability of their agricultural base, as the environmental archaeology of ancient civilizations makes clear. Expansionist Western industrial culture, dependent on resource-depleting, petroleum-based agriculture, is only different in terms of its global scale. If the lessons of the past are not heeded, its collapse will also be global (Weiskal 1989).

By the end of World War II, North American agriculture had become synonymous with technological efficiency and crop productivity, with an increasing reliance on monocultures. In the process, however, highly mechanized Canadian and American farms have come to depend more and more on fossil fuels, chemical fertilizers and pesticides, and borrowed capital. Yet today, these same farms are experiencing a decline in soil productivity, an increase in financial debts, and a reduction in profitability. In addition, the increasing reliance on agricultural chemicals has resulted in a growing number of dangers to both animal and human health (Reganold et al. 1990, p. 112). Moreover, in the adoption of an increasingly mechanized approach to food production, what was once seen as a mainly biological process is now regarded as an industrial process (Drengson 1986, p. 137).

Reliance on monoculture practices in agriculture, in turn, raises the issue of food security. In both Canada and Third World countries, the thrust of agricultural economics has been in the direction of progressive mechanization and crop specialization. An ever-growing percentage of these crops is derived from corporate-based seed banks that require the ongoing use of custom-designed fertilizers and pesticides. This has increased the vulnerability of plants to climatic changes and new diseases, while reducing the long-term resilience that comes from genetic variety.

The security of our food supply, and indeed of Canada's agricultural economy, is being put evermore at risk. Moreover, Canada's reliance on a few major export crops, such as canola oil and durum wheat, has already made our export markets subject to foreign protectionism. (Ironically, American farmers were being promised protection from Canada to promote free trade with Mexico.) In turn, by reducing its own agricultural crop options, Canadians have to rely more and more on imports from other countries — often of food that could be grown domestically. Indeed, the Third World, to the extent that it has retained healthy subsistence farming, could conceivably, in the long run, prove to be more resilient than Northern countries such as Canada.

Contemporary Canadian agricultural practice raises several environmental issues related to soil conservation and its productive maintenance for future generations. For example, in 1987, the combined effects of soil erosion, acidification, compaction, and salinization (largely because of cultivation, fertilization, and irrigation practices) may have cost Canadian growers almost $1.4 billion through reduced crop yields and increased production costs (Environment Canada 1987, p. 25).

In turn, the use of farm chemicals and resultant depositing of topsoil in ditches, streams, and rivers has resulted in sediment damage to inland lakes and waterways, recreational fishing losses, and increased water treatment and dredging costs. Surface and groundwater contamination by pesticides and the loss of wetlands and other wildlife habitat are also growing concerns (Environment Canada 1987, p. 25).

In 1984, the Senate Standing Committee on Agriculture, Fisheries and Forestry released a report on the declining quality of Canadian soils. Entitled *Soil at Risk: Canada's Eroding Future,* the 129-page document warned that soil degradation costs Canadian farmers at least $1 billion a year in lost production. Moreover, decreasing soil quality threatens agricultural land in every province. Even though soil degradation across the country appears in different forms, it produces similar results: the disappearance of nutrient-rich topsoil and lower crop yields. For example, in some areas of the Prairies, excessive cultivation and herbicide use have lowered crop productivity as much as 75 percent.

Contemporary agriculture also raises several social issues, among them are the following:

✦ The crushing debt burden;

✦ The rapid disappearance of the family farm;

✦ The loss of agricultural land to encroaching urban development, transportation networks, airports, and industrial parks; and

✦ The effects of decades of government policies.

Currently, economic difficulties on the farm threaten more farmers with bankruptcy than at any time since the Great Depression (Brown 1987, p. 122). The concept of food as a commodity and related policies encouraging expansion, increased production, and increased capital inputs have contributed to the financial crisis in Canada's farming communities (Nikiforuk 1988, pp. 36–47).

In Canada, farmers are well over $20.7 billion in debt; the Prairie farm debt totaled $13 billion ($88 thousand per farm) in 1987 (Penner 1988) and in British Columbia the debt load of farmers had reached $1.2 billion by the mid-1980s (Drengson 1986, p. 135). It is estimated that 44 thousand Canadian farms, or about one-sixth of the total, are already insolvent despite the growth in government aid from $1.1 billion in 1981 to $3.8 billion in 1988 (Science Council of Canada 1992, p. 14), totaling about $17 billion over the last decade (Mahood 1991). During the past decade, 4 258 farmers went under as a result of bankruptcy; over this same period, the total farm debt exceeded the annual value of cash receipts (Science Council of Canada 1992, p. 14). Because of the current international subsidy wars — which have slashed commodity prices, sending wheat, for example, to a 20-year low of $2 a bushel — the situation is only expected to get worse. While grain prices plunge, the cost of fuel, machinery, seed, and fertilizer — everything needed to farm — keeps rising.

Between 1981 and 1986, over 55 thousand hectares of rural land were lost to urbanization in 70 Canadian cities with populations over 25 thousand. Moreover, land with prime capability to produce crops accounted for almost 60 percent of all land converted to urban use (Warren et al. 1989). For example, in British Columbia, 80 percent of the wetlands in the Fraser River Delta have been taken from agriculture (Environment Canada 1986). Once land has been modified for urban purposes, it is essentially unavailable for alternative agricultural purposes.

Canadian agriculture consumes vast quantities of fresh water, fuel, and petrochemicals — the last through herbicides, pesticides, and fertilizers. It also consumes huge quantities of pharmaceuticals in the form of antibiotics and hormones (Drengson 1986, p. 136). Throughout the latter half of this century, agriculture has been under pressure to increase both the average farm size and the average farmer output in order to chase an ever-decreasing margin that would pay the farmer a fair return on investment and time. This has encouraged the dropping of more complex cropping techniques, such as timed planting, crop rotation, and diversified farming, in favour of specialized, chemically treated, large-scale monocultures. Increasingly, farmers, like their counterparts in forestry, have adopted an industrial approach to agriculture.

Consequently, modern agriculture requires large inputs of industrial products to achieve high production levels. For example, since 1941, the number of Canadian farms has decreased by 60 percent and the output has increased by 175 percent (Science Council of Canada 1992, p. 14). Yet, the prices of these inputs have increased dramatically over the past decade. This, combined with low farm-produce prices, has contributed to widespread financial distress. The production of food has become almost totally dependent on oil and gas, not only to provide chemicals and machinery now used on the farm but also to process and distribute farm products. Moreover, when the off-farm activities of the agricultural system are taken into account, such as transportation, food processing, food packaging, and distribution, then the ratio of energy input per energy output becomes even more inefficient (Gever et al. 1989, p. 281).

There is mounting concern about pesticide safety and soil degradation, especially as the long-term effects of agricultural chemicals on human health, the soil, and the environment are not well known. During the past decade, a growing number of "traditional" farmers have been experimenting with alternative farming techniques and methods emphasizing long-term social and financial sustainability. This is partly due to the high costs of the inputs for traditional farming and the uncertainty of commodity prices, which has left many farmers in a financial bind. In addition, chemical inputs seem to be losing their effectiveness while potentially jeopardizing the health of those who handle these hazardous chemicals (Wilde 1984, p. 183). Some farmers are motivated by the personal benefits of "greater independence, personal safety and satisfaction"

(Robinson 1986, p. 9), by a growing public demand for "organic" food products, and by the goal of long-term stewardship of the land for future generations.

During this century, the trend of farming has been toward larger, less diversified farms; higher chemical inputs; and the resulting environmental degradation, increasing debt loads, and demise of the family farm and rural communities. From 1971 to 1991, farms over 647 hectares in size grew in proportion from 3.2 to 10.1 percent in Manitoba, from 9.1 to 19.3 percent in Saskatchewan, and from 8.6 to 13 percent in Alberta.

Although conventional technologies have achieved dramatic increases in short-term food production, they have done so by increasing long-term social and environmental costs: soil degradation, the loss of arable land, the use of an increasingly controlled and select number of plant species, and an increasing reliance on chemicals. This trend has been abetted by decades of government and industry research that has fostered methods that increase production and mask diversity rather than encourage agriculture's dependence on the natural ecosystem's heterogenous characteristics. As a result, the conventional farmer has been forced "to emulate the factory manager by standardizing procedures and technology to achieve uniform results in mass quantities" (Bidwell 1986, p. 318).

Consequently, a number of critics have called for alternative agricultural practices — ones that are sustainable insofar as they would tend to maintain agricultural resources as renewable resources and begin to solve the problems inherent in conventional agriculture. These less capital-intensive techniques tend to evoke disdain from many professional agrologists because they seem to be technologically backward and seem to challenge a professional tradition. Indeed, critics of the dominant agricultural model are viewed by proponents as "against technology, politically radical, and somewhat softheaded" (Wilde 1984, p. 184). There is, however, a growing realization that the status quo is not sustainable, which means that new and creative alternatives are now required.

## Forestry in British Columbia:
## An Industry in Crisis

British Columbia's total forestland area is about 51.2 million hectares, or over half the province (Forestry Canada 1990, p. 75). However, only about half of that area is currently perceived as forestland that is both accessible and commercially viable. About half of the total Canadian volume of timber comes from British Columbia and one-third of Canada's direct forest industry jobs. Direct industry jobs peaked in British Columbia during 1979 at 95 thousand; declining to 75 thousand during the recession of 1982. In 1990, there were about 85 thousand direct industry jobs accounting for some $3 billion a year in wages. Indeed, forestry is responsible for about one-quarter of the province's gross domestic product (GDP) — direct, indirect, and induced (Travers 1990).

By the early 1990s, the provincial forest economy was facing a serious crisis. Jobs continued to be lost as a result of the high Canadian dollar, a North American economic recession, and a rapidly diminishing supply of quality old-growth timber. Consequently, in an effort to remain globally competitive, vast quantities of timber have been sold abroad at what critics claim remains well below the real market value. In turn, the BC forest companies have tried to cut costs by shutting down unprofitable mills and by mechanization — both of which have resulted in a reduced labour force. For example, in 1950, 1 thousand cubic metres of timber generated two jobs; in 1989, it generated one. Indeed, employment in the BC timber industry has been dropping at a rate of approximately 2 thousand jobs per year. By comparison, in 1984, Switzerland was able to generate 11 times the number of jobs; New Zealand, 5 times the number of jobs; and the United States, 3.5 times the number of jobs per thousand cubic metres of timber (Hammond 1991, pp. 78–80).

These disparities continue despite dramatic increases in harvest levels. Since 1911, British Columbia has logged some 2.5 billion cubic metres of wood, but half of this has been cut since 1977. The annual cut in 1990 was 74.3 million cubic metres on Crown forestland, well above the government's own estimated long-run sustained yield target of 59 million cubic metres per year (Travers 1992, p. 39). This figure jumps to 89 million cubic metres if timber harvested on private lands is also taken into account. Moreover, this figure is only the wood that has been accounted for or "scaled." It does not take into consideration the vast amounts of timber that are damaged and then left during the harvesting procedure, for which government records do not exist.

According to a recent federal report on the state of the environment, on the coast of British Columbia, which is the most productive timber area, there is about 16 years of accessible old growth remaining at current industry cutting rates (Environment Canada 1992). Industry representatives were quick to deny this figure, claiming that Environment Canada obtained much of its data from the Sierra Club of Western Canada. However, the ongoing liquidation of the ancient temperate rain forests and the current attempt to replace them by managed, monoculture, tree farms has intensified the growing conflict among competing interest groups: environmentalists, loggers, forest companies, and indigenous people. Consequently, for an increasing number of British Columbians, the current forest practices are both

◆ **Environmentally unsustainable** — The forest industry has been treating forestry as a single-sector industry and has focused almost exclusively on economic profits to the detriment and virtual exclusion of other forest values, including the myriad forest-dependent species and the ecological processes that created the trees; and

◆ **Socially unsustainable** — Many of British Columbia's 103 forestry-dependent communities have been subjected to the cycles of boom and bust common to single-industry towns; as well, increasing mechanization has led, in recent years, to massive job layoffs.

The switch to younger second-growth timber, referred to as the "fall-down effect," will pose massive problems for BC's major industry. While the supply lasts, tight growth rings and few knots make BC's old-growth lumber stronger and more reliable than second-growth timber, but that quality comes at a price.

Much of this old-growth timber is located in mountains and other scarcely accessible areas that are ecologically highly sensitive and prime wilderness–recreation regions, making harvesting costs among the world's highest. By contrast, states such as Georgia and Alabama increasingly rely on plantation operations to raise trees such as southern pine. This use is comparable to second-growth Douglas-fir, and can be produced in about a third of the time. Moreover, these southern states have the advantage of much lower harvesting and labour costs than British Columbia and enjoy relative proximity to the densely populated northeastern states. In turn, the BC pulp and paper industry is in a state of upheaval, in part because of recent provincial environmental regulations calling for a sizable reduction in the amount of organochlorine effluents. This is intensified by European markets, which are demanding a move away from chlorine-bleached pulp and forest products that originate from clear-cutting, as well as North American newspapers, which are using higher levels of recycled newsprint.

## The Need to Distinguish Between Ecological "Capital" and "Interest"

Sustainable economic growth is an oxymoron if it is couched in terms of the values and goals of the expansionist world view. If sustainable development is equated with sustained growth, the capacity of the environment to sustain itself will become progressively more difficult and, when pressed beyond its limits, eventually impossible. This thesis can be best put in terms of systems theory and its application.

For hundreds of millions of years, the planetary system has been dominated by the naturally regulating processes of countless numbers of interacting biotic and abiotic subsystems. In turn, the planet's ecosystems have been held in a relative position of "steady state," or dynamic tension and equilibrium. This is accomplished by self-regulating (or "negative feedback") mechanisms that correct deviations from the given normal state.

In contrast, contemporary economic systems, whether of the free-market or state-owned variety, are dominated by mechanisms designed to increase the size and scope of the economies. In other words, they are dominated by "positive feedbacks" that amplify deviations from the existing conditions.

Hence, the significance attached to increases in a country's GNP. It is here that the two systems have collided. Economic systems everywhere keep growing, but the ecosystems in which they are embedded do not. As a result, the consumption of ecological resources threatens — now as never before — to exceed sustainable rates of biological production. This occurs, of course, while we continue to deplete, at an ever-accelerating rate, the Earth's nonrenewable resources. Moreover, it is important to realize that production in the economy has been typically and traditionally predicated on the production of "natural capital" in the ecosphere. Indeed, the ongoing growth of GNP has historically been dependent on the ability to exploit and diminish vast quantities of biophysical capital.

In short, the expansionist economic model is driven by the accelerating depletion of ecological resources and their conversion for consumption. This system continues to curtail the opportunities for future generations to live off the natural "interest" of our forests, agricultural soils, land, and fisheries. In addition, overexploitation is worsened by pollution and the by-products of economic activity, which further impair the remaining productivity of all the planet's ecosystems.

This situation is illustrated in Figure 2, which focuses on the flows of energy and resources through a societal system. Figure 2 depicts what is described as a one-way or "throwaway" society — as found in most industrialized economies — a society that is based on maximizing the flows of energy and matter. This process results in rapidly converting the energy and products of the ecosystem to an entropic state: to waste heat, trash, and pollution. This type of society can be sustained indefinitely, but only with essentially infinite supplies of natural resources and energy and an infinite capacity on the part of the environment to absorb the resulting heat and waste by-products. As neither of these "infinites" exists, however, the throwaway society cannot continue indefinitely.

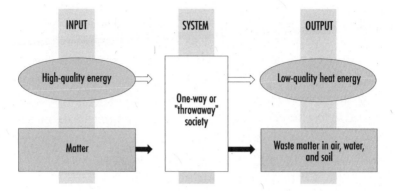

Figure 2. Energy and resource flow in a "throwaway" society: open arrows, energy; solid arrows, resources (adapted from Miller 1988).

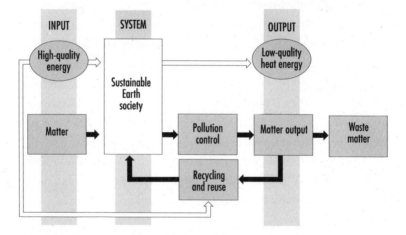

Figure 3. Energy and resource flow in a sustainable society: open arrows, energy; solid arrows, resources (adapted from Miller 1988).

Like other nations, Canada is finite in its resources and waste-absorption capacity. Hence, neither sustained nor sustainable development or growth based on prevailing patterns of consumptive resource use is possible. By contrast, Figure 3 depicts how energy and resources can be used to create a society that is more sustainable.

As William Rees (1992) argues, two key concepts are needed for sustainable development:

✦ Minimize the impacts of our activities on the environment; and

✦ Live on the interest of our natural capital.

In turn, a sustainable society is based on reusing and recycling renewable natural resources. It does not use renewable resources faster than they can be replenished by natural processes. It conserves energy. This kind of society also increases pollution control. It deliberately lowers the rate at which matter and energy resources are used so that the environment is not overloaded and the resources are not depleted. Only by these means can socioeconomic systems remain viable in the long run and, as a consequence, allow development that is both qualitative and sustainable.

The carrying capacity of the Earth is more or less constant. It is determined by such factors as the availability of nutrients and the photosynthetic efficiency by which plants convert sunlight to available energy. Consequently, by increasing the level of consumption, we are also reducing the capacity of the planet to support other species. This, in turn, reduces the ability of the environment to support humans. In this simple truth lies the essence of our environmental crisis. We have not only been living off our ecological interest but also consuming the capital, and the rate at which we are doing so is increasing year by year. As we have seen, this is being demonstrated in Canada through forestry practices in British Columbia and the loss of productive soils and farmland. It has also been witnessed in the dramatic depletion of both Atlantic and Pacific fish stocks.

To maintain their affluent standard of living, Canadians, in turn, have been "appropriating" the carrying capacities not only of Canada's ecosystems but also of other ecosystems throughout the world. Why is this?

✦ First of all, Canada has a cold climate and the productivity of the land is relatively low.

✦ Second, we have been using many of the most productive lands to extract resources that we sell to other countries — often with little value added.

✦ Third, some of the most productive lands in other countries have been appropriated to generate products and finished goods that are imported into Canada and other rich countries.

✦ Fourth, we use vast areas of land to store water for energy production, both for our own use and for export.

As well, Canadians use more fossil fuels, on a per-capita basis, than any other country in the world. As Rees (1992) points out: "We are among the worst offenders in terms of drawing down the world's natural capital." Indeed, Canada has been a wealthy country because we have been converting our natural capital into financial capital. Moreover, we have been reluctant to reinvest our wealth in the maintenance of our natural resources, which we will need to achieve sustainability (Rees 1992).

# Chapter 5

# Toward Sustainability

*A growing economy is getting bigger; a developing econ-
omy is getting better. An economy can therefore develop
without growing or grow without developing.*

— Herman Daly

## The Emergence of an Ecological World View

The goal of sustained development is fundamental to the North's
traditional adherence to the concept of "growth." Underlying this is
the assumption of never-ending "superabundance." However,
growth-oriented economics cannot continue without conflicting with
the realities of ecological systems.

The evolution of the planet and its resources has taken place
over millions of years. Global ecosystems have functioned on the
dominance of negative-feedback mechanisms and self-limiting factors, thereby maintaining the dynamic equilibrium of biological
processes and physical resources. In contrast, the expansionist world
view functions on the basis of positive feedback and self-amplifying
behaviour. This has had the effect of depleting the planet's overall
natural endowment and the ability of biological systems to ade-
quately renew themselves. Human activities associated with such a
perspective and behaviour have resulted in forms of "development"
that for three reasons, at least, have become unsustainable:

+ The continual and accelerating consumption and depletion of
nonrenewable resources;

+ The use of renewable resources at a faster rate than their rate
of regeneration; and

✦ The cumulative degradation of the environment in terms of the loss of natural systems and ecological processes, which, in turn, has led to the widespread and increasing extinction of species and destruction of genetic diversity.

An ecological world view is based on the concept of the world as a myriad of interlocked systems and interacting processes. Human activities and development strategies will have to take account of this emerging perception. However, development in Canada, no less than elsewhere in the North, continues to be predicated on the growth ethos. This results in the positive-feedback processes in our economy — with its sophisticated technologies — continually wreaking havoc with the homeostatic ecological systems in which they are embedded.

We can continue with this feedback disequilibrium only at our increasing peril. Ecological systems have to be seen as primary and the economy has to adapt. People must understand that the economy fits into and is part of the environment, not the other way around. Except for solar energy, for all intents and purposes, the Earth is a closed system. This means that economic production is now synonymous with the consumption of resources and an overall net increase in entropy and disorder in the natural world. Whereas ecosystems are inherently self-maintaining and self-organizing — although limited according to nutrient levels and photosynthetic abilities — our economic activities have begun everywhere to exceed biological levels of sustainability (Rees 1990b).

Ultimately, our sociopolitical systems are subsystems of the larger natural environment, and the long-term viability of our human systems depends on our willingness to live within the ability of the Earth's ecosystems to repair and reproduce themselves. In short, this will entail a radical restructuring of our economic priorities as we know them today. It will require a fundamental change of attitude toward our social needs and values. Nowhere is this need more evident than in Canada's policies and practices toward its own natural resources.

## Ecology as a Subversive Science

Ecology has been termed a "subversive science" and has sometimes been used in this way (Evernden 1985, p. 5). The study of ecology in academic circles has its full quota of specialists concerned with statistical approaches and reductionist techniques (Goldsmith 1988, pp. 64–74); it has also been used as a forum from which to criticize many of the tenets underlying the modern condition. Using the study of nature to support various values and ideas that are at odds with established ones is not new, and ecology in its more radical form is just a more recent example of this kind of behaviour.

In the past 200 years of Western literature about the environment and our relationship to it, descriptions of the natural world have tended to reflect the values and biases of each period. Indeed, our perceptions of nature and how it works often tell us less about what is actually "out there" in the landscape and more about the types of mental topography, biases, and projections in our own heads. Nevertheless, the study of nature and of the "natural" has frequently been brought into service against the orthodox values of the day (Taylor 1990, pp. 174–176).

The study of ecology and the environment now goes hand in hand with the questioning of many of the common assumptions about ourselves and the state of our political and economic systems. Theories concerning the properties of ecosystems and their vulnerability to human interference are regularly used to challenge the ways in which we view our relationship to each other and the world about us. For example, the notion of "interrelatedness" and the idea that there are no discrete or isolated entities flies in the face of traditional atomistic theories. It challenges and subverts those dualisms associated with the notion that humans are somehow separate from the natural world, and that political and economic institutions can safely treat the natural environment as an external factor or an afterthought.

The modern environmental movement encompasses the values and beliefs that form the ecological world view. In attacking the fundamental assumptions of the conventional world view, various members of this movement have looked to both Western and non-Western sources for their historical and philosophical antecedents. They have found inspiration in concepts from India and China that emphasize the essential unity of human life with the rest of nature. They have also been inspired by the North American native peoples' belief in the primary value of kinship and relatedness to all life-forms and Mother Earth (Fox 1988). Others have found common ground with premodern European traditions, including many of the animistic beliefs found in early Celtic, Germanic, and Nordic societies; with the mystical traditions of Sufism and Hasidism; and with the Christian mysticism of Meister Eckhart, Teresa of Avila, and Hildegard of Bingen. In turn, it has been argued that the ecological world view is closely aligned with the nondualistic tradition of interrelatedness found in Leibniz, Hegel, and Whitehead, as well as with much of the Counter-Enlightenment and Romantic thought of the 18th and 19th centuries.

The influence of Counter-Enlightenment thought on the modern environmental movement has yet to be fully appreciated. Although Counter-Enlightenment resists simple definition, the rise to prominence in the West of Newtonian and Enlightenment values and assumptions during the 18th century led to a series of reactions. These reactions protested a world view that sought to rationalize and mechanize both humans and nature within the overall image of the universe as some "Great Machine." The impact of Newtonian science on the development of our modern expansionist world view was enormous. And even though Newtonian science — certainly for Newton — had welded the spiritual order to that of nature, it also instigated a world view that became progressively divorced from intrinsic spirituality and values.

By the end of the 18th century, the values and assumptions underlying Newtonian mechanics were gaining wide acceptance among leading Western intellectuals (Cassirer 1951, pp. 3–36). With the separation of the subjective knower from the objective known, as well as the separation of facts from values, very little could actually be said about anything not physically measurable. It was a world in which quantities rather than qualities really mattered. Thus, values, instincts, emotions, and all that could not be measured or clearly scrutinized under the light of reason were thought to be of secondary importance.

## Counter-Enlightenment and Romantic Thought

Advocates of Counter-Enlightenment opposed the doctrines of rationalism (Berlin 1982). Romanticism — as part of the stream of dissident Counter-Enlightenment thought that emerged in the late 18th and early 19th centuries — challenged the intellectual orthodoxy of the time that some felt was straightjacketing life in the narrow bounds of reason and geometry. As opposed to the primacy given to reason and science, romantics stressed the importance of the nonrational, the emotional, and the instinctual. If the overall societal trend in the West was toward the urban and the technological, the romantics reacted by celebrating the world of nature and all that appeared natural and not artificial.

By the end of the 18th century, the mainstream of modern thought had tended to sever knower from known, spirit from matter, God from nature. But the romantics tried to unify these apparent dualisms, usually through an organicist world view and a denial of the atomistic and reductionist tendencies inherent in Newtonian and Enlightenment thought. And if nature, from the perspective of mechanistic science, had lost all spiritual and intrinsic worth, romantic writers attempted to counter this metaphysical loss by pointing to an essential unity between the supernatural and the natural realms.

During the 19th century, American transcendentalists, such as Thoreau and Emerson, followed this general theme by asserting that individuals know universal truths through their inner light of intuition and their empathetic communion with nature. They believed that the state, with its institutionalized forms of authority, stands in the way of these truths. In many ways, Thoreau's *Walden* was an exercise in political anarchism enabling Thoreau to use "nature" as an arena from which to stand outside and thereby criticize the existing polis, including many of its associated values: the status of civil authority; the Lockean values of ownership, property, and scarcity; and society's conformity and bondage to false needs, to name a few. For Thoreau, as for other transcendentalist writers, the appreciation of nature was inextricably linked to an ideological attack on the existing status quo.

## Against the Current: "Righteous Management Conservation"

Deeply influenced by the writings of Emerson and the transcendentalists, John Muir (1838–1914) led a series of attacks on the excesses and vulgarities of modernity's expansionist world view versus the sanctity of nature, which he at one point described as "a mirror reflecting the Creator." Foreshadowing the later work of Aldo Leopold, Muir argued for the adoption of an environmental land ethic that would recognize all natural objects and living things as ends in themselves. In doing so, he was rejecting a basic tenet of modernity that had come to view nature primarily in utilitarian and economic terms. This view was to put him increasingly at odds with his contemporary, Gifford Pinchot, as well as the values that dominated North American society at the turn of the century. As a founder of the Sierra Club in 1892, John Muir had also laid the foundations of what was to become known as the "preservationist" or "righteous management" school of conservation (Devall and Sessions 1985; Turner 1987).

The conservation movement was a reaction to the excesses and wastefulness of an expanding industrial society. But, by the turn of the century, conservationists were viewing the problem from two very different world views. Thus, the ideological rift between John Muir and Gifford Pinchot reflected the schism between the Counter-Enlightenment/Romantic and the more pragmatic Enlightenment traditions. The Counter-Enlightenment/Romantic antecedents of the conservation movement have already been outlined. Its characteristic stance on the natural world is an integral part of the ecological world view — in summary:

✦ **The universe is an interrelated totality, with all its parts interconnected and interlocked** — A corollary to this is the rejection of those dualistic and atomistic categories in the Newtonian mechanistic perspective: for example, the epistemological separation of the subjective knower from the objective known, and the radical separation of facts (quantities) from values (qualities).

✦ **Nature is intrinsically valuable; animals, trees, or rocks all have worth and value "in themselves" regardless of what other value they may have to human beings** — This is an essentially nonanthropocentric perspective and a rejection of the typically quantitative approach to nature, with its emphasis on viewing the natural world primarily in economic and utilitarian terms.

✦ **Nature is both a physical and a symbolic forum from which to criticize modern society** — Human beings are afforded an opportunity to actualize their own inner spiritual, aesthetic, and moral sensibilities. In turn, physical nature — especially wilderness — is a benchmark against which the state of human society may be judged. Consequently, large areas of the natural world should be preserved and protected against human interference.

## Green Alternatives

In recent years, the ecological view has been further articulated in the writings of "deep ecologists," "ecofeminists," and "social ecologists" — all of whom find in "ecology" a forum from which to criticize the dominant values and assumptions underlying modern society. In turn, such criticisms have become the basis for an emerging "green" politics throughout Europe and North America.

In keeping with the Counter-Enlightenment and Romantic perspective, deep ecologists such as Arne Naess have called for the recognition of two fundamental principles: self-realization and biocentric equality.

Self-realization here goes beyond the egocentric individualism typical of Western culture to an awareness of one's ultimate inseparability and organic wholeness with the nonhuman world. In turn, there is the recognition that all organisms and entities in the ecosphere are endowed with intrinsic worth and comprise part of an interrelated web of life (Devall and Sessions 1985).

Ecofeminism, like deep ecology, is rooted in an organic perspective of the natural world; but it also seeks to address the hierarchical and dominance relationships that it sees as endemic to patriarchy — much of which has emanated from and been perpetuated by religious dogmas, especially in the West. As such, ecofeminism moves outside the Counter-Enlightenment framework and finds much in common with the egalitarian and antiauthoritarian tradition of socialism. Indeed, ecofeminism equates the ongoing domination of nature with the ongoing domination of women, arguing that both are systemically related (Salleh 1984, pp. 339–345).

Similarly, social ecologists, such as Murray Bookchin, have argued that sexism, ageism, racism, and militarism — indeed, all forms of human domination — are intimately related to the issues of ecology. For Bookchin, as long as various modes of hierarchy and domination continue in human society, then "the project of dominating nature will continue to exist and inevitably lead our planet to ecological extinction" (Bookchin 1980, p.76). Bookchin's model for "social ecology" finds its roots in such sources as the anarchical writings of Peter Kropotkin and the utopian perspective of Charles Fourier. Criticizing modernity from outside the Counter-Enlightenment perspective, it prescribes a social order that is essentially egalitarian, decentralized, and communal in its orientation. It criticizes the "concept of the domination of nature by humanity by eliminating the domination of human by human" (Bookchin 1980, p. 77).

A somewhat similar dissident strain of political decentralism and egalitarianism, but from a socialist tradition, is epitomized in the late 19th-century writings of William Morris. His utopian *News from Nowhere* advocates a philosophy of "small is beautiful," in which humanity is seen as an integral part of nature in a relationship that is active but loving, and in which technology is subordinated to the values of fellowship and beauty. Indeed, Morris' criticism of modernity makes a connection between the desire to dominate nature and a social system that promotes the domination of one human by another.

Increasingly, the proponents of an emerging ecological world view have found an ally in general systems theory. This approach emerged, during the first half of the 20th century, from the study of biology and cybernetics. It is a rejection of the reductionism inherent in mechanistic science. Studying the various ways in which physical, biological, and social systems are able to maintain and transform themselves as "dissipative structures far-from-equilibrium," the systems approach views the universe as a systemic hierarchy (or "holarchy") or organized complexity — as myriad wholes within wholes, all of them interconnected and interacting (Prigogine and Stengers 1984; Laszlo 1987). In the past decade, this perspective has also appeared in terms of the "Gaia" hypothesis, which attempts to explain the Earth and its living organisms in terms of a single, indivisible, self-regulating process (Lovelock 1988). Indeed, this theory has given added urgency to the belief that current human perturbations, grounded in an expansionist world view, all threaten Gaia's health and the life therein.

## The Ecological World View as a Mirror Image

The obvious weakness of the ecological world view as it has so far emerged is that — like the Counter-Enlightenment and Romantic traditions in which it is largely, though not exclusively, rooted — it has tended to be the "mirror image" of the expansionist world view. In this sense, it also has its own form of dualistic thinking as well as remaining subject to the contradictions and inadequacies of the world view it opposes. This tendency is illustrated in an article by Stephen Cotgrove and Andrew Duff in which they attempt to contrast the "dominant social paradigm" with what they regard as attributes of an "alternative environmental paradigm" (Table 1).

Similar lists of oppositional values contrasting the ecological world view with the expansionist world view have become common. In placing itself in opposition to the underlying values of industrial

Table 1. Two opposing social paradigms.

| Dominant Social Paradigm | Alternative Environmental Paradigm |
|---|---|
| **Core values** | |
| Material (economic growth) | Nonmaterial (self-actualization) |
| Natural environment valued as resource | Natural environment intrinsically valued |
| Domination over nature | Harmony with nature |
| **Economy** | |
| Market forces | Public interest |
| Risk and reward | Safety |
| Differentials | Incomes related to need (egalitarian) |
| Individual self-help | Collective, social provision |
| **Society** | |
| Centralized | Public interest |
| Large-scale | Safety |
| Associational | Communal |
| Ordered | Flexible |
| **Nature** | |
| Ample reserves | Earth's resources limited |
| Nature hostile or neutral | Nature benign |
| Environment controllable | Nature delicately balanced |
| **Knowledge** | |
| Confidence in science and technology | Limits to science |
| Rationality of means | Rationality of ends |
| Separation of fact and value, thought and feeling | Integration of fact and value |

Source: Cotgrove and Duff (1980, p. 341).

society, the environmental movement has already taken its necessary first step. To help a new world view emerge, more of its proponents must now be willing to take time to identify, clarify, and evaluate the underlying assumptions of the existing dominant world view. To fail to do so is to risk being co-opted by the values of the older model.

There is an ongoing need to challenge the dominant expansionist position and be distanced from it. In many respects, protagonists of the environmental movement, who have embraced the Counter-

Enlightenment and Romantic traditions, can step back into "nature" and critically assess "civilization" from another perspective. They also assert that technology must be redesigned to promote human values and fit acceptable cultural and environmental limits. The very notion of an "appropriate" technology calls into question the "inappropriateness" of those technological values, such as the "quick fix," that currently permeate the modern world (Winner 1986).

Although aligning oneself with "nature" may be a necessary first step in an alternative world view, it is not by itself a viable option for the future. In reacting to the Enlightenment assumptions of an expansionist world view, Counter-Enlightenment has tended to define itself simply in opposition to these very assumptions. To the extent that the ecological world view, around which the environmental movement coalesces, is an extension of this historical tradition, it remains an incomplete perspective. As the ecological world view matures, it should include contributions from other social traditions, especially the communitarian left. Crucial here are theories of social equality and the liberating possibilities of more environmentally benign technology. However, as the political right, from Malthus to Hitler, have also called for a return to the "natural order," the ecological world view should remain watchful and critical.

The great strength of the ecological world view is its ability to criticize the dominant values and assumptions underlying modern Western society. This is particularly important now when we are facing growing national and international environmental problems and only answering them with sustainable development.

## Sustainable Development: An Elusive Concept

What is sustainable development? It has been argued that it has been subsumed under two conflicting world views: the expansionist and the ecological. Sustainable development has become a myth, a metaphor, a metamorphosis, and a menace.

✦ It has become a **myth** very much along the lines of a utopia. It is the vision of a new Eden and a call for a society based on harmonious social patterns, interdependencies, and mutual reciprocities, as well as the intrinsic value and sacredness of all life-forms.

✦ It is a **metaphor** for our ability to transform our political, economic, and social institutions to what is both socially, as well as environmentally, sustainable.

✦ It is also an image of **metamorphosis** insofar as it represents the need to transform ourselves collectively to a new and emergent level of organization in dynamic equilibrium with the natural systems to which we are attached; in other words, learn to live off the interest of nature and to be able to bequeath to future generations a similar or greater level of environmental capital and assets than we have received (Pearse et al. 1989, p. 3).

✦ Finally, sustainable development is a **menace** as it has been co-opted by individuals and institutions to perpetuate many of the worst aspects of the expansionist model under the masquerade of something new.

Maurice Strong, one of Canada's two representatives on the Brundtland Commission, has mused that sustainable development is in danger of becoming the fig leaf behind which business hides — we might also include governments and individuals. Certainly, this was the impression that many observers were left with at the conclusion of the Rio Earth Summit. Although the Summit was billed as the best chance to put our planet on a course toward sustainable development, it failed miserably in going beyond the realm of rhetoric to the implementation of actual concrete solutions.

Indeed, the representatives from Northern nations largely ignored social justice and equity issues and were unwilling to face up to the sorts of fundamental sociopolitical changes that will likely be necessary for any transition toward a sustainable world. Moreover, the Rio Earth Summit failed to recognize that, for many, the current environmental crisis is essentially a cultural crisis. Indeed, the idea of sustainable development that nongovernmental organization

(NGO) representatives entertained was more often than not at odds with that of the panelists representing business and government. This merely served to underscore the thesis that people are tending to talk at cross-purposes to one another, often from the perspective of two conflicting and incompatible world views.

Sustainable development is hard to define precisely. Like the horizon it has a tendency to recede whenever one attempts to discover its boundaries. Yet, for an increasing number of people in Canada, and elsewhere, discussions about sustainable development have become a platform for an alternative world view and an ongoing critique of current national and international policies and values as they affect the long-term viability of both social and natural systems. The call for sustainable development is a useful moral position the public can use to push politicians into accepting fundamental structural changes that may be prerequisites for our collective survival in the coming century. Meanwhile, an historical understanding of the basic differences between the expansionist and emerging ecological world views will help us to realize more fully the implications of the central issue: How can we develop both environmental and societal sustainability?

# Chapter 6

# Principles of Sustainable Development

*Development is a whole; it is an integral, value-loaded, cultural process; it encompasses the natural environment, social relations, education, production, consumption, and well-being.*

— Dag Hammarskjöld Foundation

Sustainable development in the future is only possible if we are willing to maintain our natural capital assets. Indeed, Canada's social wealth has resulted in the impoverishment of our natural wealth. We have failed to use this wealth to create adequate levels of secondary or tertiary industry, which would enable us to maintain a level of financial prosperity and funnel resources back to maintain our natural resource base. Instead, we are being increasingly forced to liquidate our natural endowment in the name of economies of scale and a federal government's commitment to free trade and global competitiveness.

It has been pointed out that sustainable development remains an elusive concept. Indeed, to a large extent, it may be thought of as a vision for transforming our currently growth-oriented socio-economic system to one that is predicated on an emerging ecological world view's vision of environmental sustainability and social justice. As such, it remains an ideal. However, within this perspective, there is a growing body of literature that agrees on a broad set of principles for sustainability to guide us toward these goals. For instance, there is increasing recognition that our political and economic institutions must be seen as subsystems of our planetary ecology and be informed by its limitations and requirements. In turn, specific ecological components from the emerging ecological world view that underlie these principles include the following (Bailey 1990):

✦ The value of biological diversity;

✦ Ecological limits on human activity;

✦ The intimately intertwined and systemic nature of the planet's abiotic and biotic components;

✦ The thermodynamic irreversibility of natural processes; and

✦ The recognition of the dynamic, constantly evolving, and often unpredictable properties of natural systems.

Moreover, it is generally agreed that environmental sustainability must be built on long-term economic and social sustainability. These principles are summarized in this chapter (also see British Columbia 1992, pp. 14–18).

## Sustainable Environment

A healthy environment is the foundation on which a sound economy and society depends. The essential role that ecosystems play in supporting our society establishes an environmental imperative that must be respected in all land, resource, and economic decisions. Our priority must be to maintain natural systems for present and future generations.

✦ **Conserve life-support services** — These are the ecological processes that sustain the productivity, adaptability, and capacity for the renewal of lands, water, air, and all life on Earth. These processes include maintaining the chemical balance of the planet; stabilizing the climate; recycling nutrients; breaking down pollutants and cleansing air and water; stabilizing water flow; forming and regenerating soil; and supplying food and a suitable habitat for all species.

✦ **Conserve biological diversity in genes, species, and eco-systems** — This encompasses the variety of different species of plants, animals, and other organisms; the variety of different genetic stocks in each species; and the variety of different ecosystems. There are three reasons for conserving the diversity of nature: as a matter of **principle** — all species have a right to exist by virtue of their intrinsic value; as a matter of **survival** — the diversity of life is needed for optimizing the biotic and abiotic conditions for the continuation of life; and as a matter of **economic benefit** — the diversity of nature is the ultimate source of food, raw materials, and many other goods and services; hence, we must strive to respect the integrity of natural systems and to restore previously degraded environments.

✦ **Attempt to anticipate and prevent adverse environmental impacts** — When making land and resource decisions, adopt the precautionary approach, exercise caution and special concern for natural values, and recognize that human understanding of nature is incomplete.

✦ **Practice full cost accounting** — Ensure that environmental and social costs are accounted for in land, resource use, species depletion, and economic decisions.

✦ **Recognize our responsibility to protect the global environment** — We must exercise stewardship, reduce consumption to sustainable levels, avoid importing or exporting ecological stresses, and help meet the global challenge of sustainably supporting the human population.

✦ **Respect the intrinsic value of nature** — The environment must be protected for human uses and enjoyment.

These could be the most critical criteria for ecological and societal sustainability alike. It is indeed a sobering thought to recall that in this century the planetary population has quadrupled beyond the figure reached by our species in the previous 3 million years or more. Within only a further half century it will have increased sixfold. This is especially a concern considering the argument that the human impact on the ecosystems of the planet is the product of the number of people multiplied by how much energy and raw materials each person and social group uses and wastes.

Obviously, an excessive impact can be caused by a few people consuming a lot, or a lot of people consuming a little. Consequently, even though the Earth's ability to renew itself and absorb wastes can be enhanced by careful management, there is a limit. So, what is the maximum number of people the planet can support and at what level of living? What is the optimal number to ensure that societies on every continent can not only satisfy their basic needs but also enjoy a quality of life, however defined in future decades? Have we already passed both the optimal level of societal sustainability and the maximum level of long-term environmental sustainability?

Although we have yet to determine these precise limits, there are increasing indicators of what can and cannot be done, and what stage human society is at. The signs are not all that good.

## Sustainable Economy

Our ability to sustain a quality environment depends on our ability to foster a strong and sustainable economy. Such an economy is more efficient and derives greater social benefits from the use of fewer environmental assets. In addition, a sustainable economy can provide the means for increased environmental protection and conservation, while offering society alternatives to undue exploitation of natural resources.

✦ **Strive to define economic development** — Not in terms of growth per se, but in terms of the increasing capacity to meet human needs and improve the quality of human life, while using a constant level of physical resources.

✦ **Encourage diversified economic development** — Development that increases employment and other benefits derived from a given stock of resources.

✦ **Encourage efficient economic development** — Development that reduces wastes and makes efficient use of resources.

✦ **Ensure that all renewable resources are used in a manner that is sustainable over the long term** — Renewable resources include soils, wild and domesticated organisms, and ecosystems. Renewable resources should not be used at rates that exceed their capacity to renew themselves.

✦ **Ensure that nonrenewable resources are not exhausted and enough is left for future generations** — Nonrenewable resources should not be used at rates that exceed our capacity to create substitutes for them.

✦ **Economic activity should work within the capacity of ecosystems** — It should strive to assimilate or process the wastes associated with such activity.

✦ **Stimulate environmentally sound economic activity** — Through a combination of educational awareness, political and legal measures, and economic instruments.

✦ **Encourage attitudinal and behavioural change** — These profound economic changes can only take place as a result of altered behaviours and attitudes.

The concept of carrying capacity is often defined as "the maximum population that can be supported in a given habitat without permanently damaging the ecosystem" (Rees 1990b). However, in terms of human life, the issue of "quality of life" must be taken into account (Figure 4). How individuals and communities define this will help to determine their impact on the larger environment.

For instance, if a community values a rich and luxurious life-style, then the carrying capacity of the environment decreases. Therefore, the definition above might be amended by substituting "the optimal population" for the phrase "the maximum population."

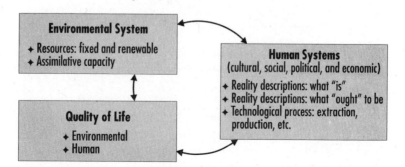

Figure 4. Carrying capacity and quality of life (adapted from Mabbutt 1985).

Consequently, carrying capacity, in terms of human systems, can be further defined as follows (Mabbutt 1985):

> *The level of human activity (including population dynamics and economic activity) that a region can sustain (including considera-tion of import and export of resources and waste residuals) at acceptable "quality-of-life" levels in perpetuity.*

A useful basis for defining "quality of life" can be found by again turning to Maslow's hierarchy of needs theory (Figure 5). Individual "quality of life" may be characterized as the extent or degree to which a person or community can satisfy this hierarchical spectrum of needs. This spectrum ranges from basic physical needs to social needs, and from ego and self-esteem needs to cultural and self-actualization (spiritual) needs.

Obviously, as increasing environmental and related constraints require Canadians to shift progressively from a consumer- to a

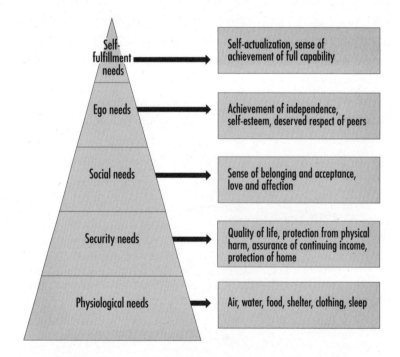

Figure 5. Maslow's hierarchy of needs theory (adapted from Mabbutt 1985).

conserver-oriented society, a redefinition of such terms as "growth" and "progress" will be needed. This redefinition process needs to include a concept of quality of life within the limitations set by a given ecosystem.

Figure 5 raises a related question: When do "needs" become "wants" or "demands"? Although behaviour patterns vary from one society to another, in the final analysis the answer to this question will be constrained or defined by the carrying capacity of the biophysical environment.

## Social Sustainability

The protection and enhancement of the environment is inextricably linked to the promotion of social equity and justice. Social equity requires that the concerns of individuals and communities be respected as environmental and economic needs are balanced.

✦ **Aim for an equitable distribution of the benefits and costs of resource use and decisions** — Ensure that the benefits and costs of resource use and environmental management are shared fairly among various communities and interest groups, between rich countries and poor countries, and between present and future generations.

✦ **Remember future generations** — Strive to ensure that the next generation is able to inherit a stock of environmental assets equal to, or possibly greater than, the stock inherited by the previous generation (Pearse et al. 1989, p. 34).

✦ **Promote a good quality of life** — This can be achieved by fostering opportunities to earn a living; obtain education and training; access social, cultural, and recreational services; and enjoy a quality environment.

✦ **Recognize that equity requires a greatly enhanced public involvement in land-use and related resource and environmental decisions** — In many ways, this would entail the decentralization of various degrees of political power "to jurisdictions that are closely linked to natural environmental regions, and the promotion of greater local and regional self-reliance"

(Robinson et al. 1990, p. 43). To be effective, this public involvement will require access to a minimal level of financial and information resources.

The Brundtland Report sets forth the idea that sustainable development "meets the needs of the present without compromising the ability of future generations to meet their own needs." What has to be determined, however, is what constitutes "essential needs." It has been argued that the planet has limited resources that cannot be expected to satisfy all of our expectations or wants. The report sets forth the following nine essential needs (WCED 1987, pp. 43–56): employment; food security and quality; clothing; energy; housing; water supply and sanitation; health care, including family planning services; education; and income, at a level at which an individual or household can afford, on a regular basis, the necessities of life.

Michael Prince, of the University of Victoria's Faculty of Human and Social Development, has suggested that in the Canadian context it would be instructive to determine to what extent the essential needs of the people of Canada are not being met. He goes on to note that we need to explore those aspirations that people have — beyond meeting their basic needs — for "an improved quality-of-life" (Prince 1992).

We might turn to the studies of specialists such as Abraham Maslow (1968), well known for his theory of the hierarchy of needs. Although one may argue with aspects of Maslow's model, it is worth noting that human fulfillment often goes well beyond the satisfaction of the essential needs listed in the Brundtland Report. In a consumer society, the actualization of "meta-needs," such as spiritual values, is often inhibited by a pervasive commitment to secondary, or even false, consumer values and perceived needs. Hence, the "born-to-shop" mentality not only helps to impoverish the natural environment but impoverishes many by denying us the experience of deeper psychological and spiritual values. The remoteness from nature in our concrete, pollution-ridden, urban jungles emphasizes this.

# The Long-Term Goals of the Ecological World View

The Brundtland Report has argued eloquently why we must reverse the current degradation of the environment, which was "first seen as mainly a problem of the rich nations and a side effect of industrial wealth [but which] has become a survival issue for developing nations" (WCED 1987, p. xi). The report points out the link between the problems and prospects of the planetary environment and those of human societies — rich and poor. But one should recognize that the report was also a political document. It had to find an acceptable compromise between the North's concern about a global demographic explosion and a rapidly deteriorating environment and the South's insistence that economic development and social opportunities must be given a higher priority than environmental protection.

At the same time, we need also recognize that, in purpose and emphasis, *Our Common Future* is anthropocentric. It places our species at the centre of the evolutionary process and, consequently, perceives and evaluates the planet's ecology in terms of human needs and values. A growing number of environmental writers find this perception not only unnecessarily limited but also, in the long run, fraught with its own danger. They call for a "common future" that is ecocentric, giving equal value and significance to all species without exception. For many, the ecological world view should include the following standards and goals:

✦ Current human interference with the nonhuman world is excessive, and the situation is rapidly worsening.

✦ Policies must therefore be changed. These policies affect basic economic, technological, and ideological structures. The resulting state of affairs will be very different from that of today.

✦ The recognition that both human and nonhuman living beings have value in themselves. Nonhuman life is intrinsically valuable regardless of its value to humans.

✦ The richness and diversity of living beings (human and nonhuman) has value in itself.

✦ Humans have no right to reduce this richness and diversity, except when it occasionally becomes necessary to satisfy vital human needs.

✦ The flourishing of human life and cultures is compatible with a substantial decrease in the global population. The flourishing of nonhuman life requires such a decrease.

✦ The appreciation of a high quality of life will have to supersede that of a high material standard of life (as measured by economic and materialistic criteria).

✦ Those who accept the foregoing points have an obligation to try to contribute to the implementation of the necessary changes.

Proceeding to this ecocentric position is, according to deep ecologists such as Arne Naess, a "long-term imperative." It is not too soon to begin to shift from our existing environmental values and goals, exemplified by the expansionist world view, to a more ecological perspective (Naess, in Devall and Sessions 1985, p. 70). As the planet's atmosphere, lithosphere, and hydrosphere can be sustained only by the interactivity of life everywhere, we must recognize the deep significance of all other life-forms, and work with them as indispensable cohabitants of a shared planet.

# Chapter 7

# The Transition
# to a Sustainable
# Canadian Society

*D*epend upon it, sir, when a man knows he is to be hanged
in a fortnight, it concentrates his mind wonderfully.
— Samuel Johnson (18th century)

Shifting from sustained to sustainable development is a fundamental
requirement for the continuing viability of our society. The expansionist world view, with its uncritical acceptance of unlimited growth
at the expense of our physical resources, should give way to a
paradigmatic strategy that recognizes and abides by the environmental limitations needed for an indefinitely sustainable society. In
addition to environmental sustainability, the shift includes economic,
demographic, and political sustainability.

## Economic Implications of a Biologically
## Sustainable Environment

The current structural difficulties of either market-driven or state-
controlled economies raise doubts about their capability to achieve
sustainable economic development. The triad of deficits, debts, and
inflation continues to bedevil the global economy, which functions
solely in terms of the expansionist world view. This triad is wreaking
havoc throughout the Third World and threatens Canada's own
longer term prospects. From a systems perspective, this is a mani-
festation of increasing perturbations throughout the global system
— the triad comprises interacting positive feedback processes

that are accelerating the destabilization of national economies everywhere. The situation will worsen as the environment itself becomes part of the syndrome.

Given our destructive resource practices, Canadians will have to repair the massive damage by engaging in restoration forestry, agriculture, and fisheries. "Restoration" means the restitution of these sectors, as nearly as possible, to their original biospheric state in terms of their biological productivity, biodiversity, and ability to absorb and recycle wastes. Federal and provincial governments must launch programs that work hand in hand with communities and individuals to restructure resource-based industries to maintain and enhance the natural capital of these sectors.

A new Canadian strategy to attain economic sustainability would advocate much greater emphasis on regional and community self-sufficiency. This approach can develop economic activities in consonance with and more sensitive to the sustainable parameters of a given region's ecology. Development projects should help to expand and stabilize the resident labour force by creating jobs within the community and aim to increase the community's decision-making input into the project. Expenditures should remain local by processing the regional resources locally, instead of exporting them for processing elsewhere (as so often happens with a variety of forestry and agricultural products). This strategy for developing greater levels of regional self-sufficiency both recognizes and takes advantage of this country's many major environmental regions, each of which possesses its own geospheric and biospheric diversity.

The Canadian economy is burdened by an extremely high and rapidly rising debt load, both at the provincial and federal levels. For example, by early 1994, the federal debt had already exceeded $640 billion, of which some $300 billion was owed to offshore interests. Despite attempts to cut back spending in provincial transfer payments and other services, annual deficits continue to remain above $30 billion. Indeed, in the past few decades, these debts increased with the commitment to unshackled growth. Under Prime Minister Mulroney's administration, massive foreign investment was encouraged in Canada, along with foreign takeovers of major

Canadian enterprises. This expansionist strategy has not generated sufficient revenue to keep pace with the ever-mounting debt load in either the private or public sector.

Unfortunately, the federal finance minister does not have many options. The federal government is under increasing pressure to raise taxes and cut spending. Yet, higher taxes on personal income and consumer goods and cuts in spending, whether by selling off Crown corporations or cutting back on expenditures to unemployment insurance and other social services, while reducing the annual deficit, will probably not eliminate it. Meanwhile, the federal debt will continue to mount. This will, in all likelihood, have the following effects: lower economic growth, both short term and long term; more foreign debt and less ability to pay for it; and less to spend on our current social programs or desperately needed environmental programs, let alone invest in new ones, even in times of prosperity.

However, neither the current finance minister nor his government can expect to resolve these wrenching long-range socio-economic questions. Increasingly, decisions affecting societal sustainability that are compatible with the superordinate requirements for sustaining the Canadian — and planetary — biophysical environment will have to be made. To the extent that these decisions are ignored or delayed, the harsher and more compelling the ecological demands will become. Concomitantly, the sooner our economic and political options will diminish.

In February 1989, scientists disclosed that the ozone layer, already punctured over the Antarctic, was now at risk in the Northern Hemisphere. The Ontario government thereupon banned the manufacture of CFCs and halons. This move pleased environmentalists, but only as a limited first step. They had earlier claimed that the Montreal Protocol was already out of date when signed, and they continued to argue that much more drastic steps must be taken quickly by the international community if the crisis was not to become a catastrophe. In this case, the importance of the environment was implicitly being recognized, by both environmentalists and Ontario politicians, whose decision had political, technological, and economic ramifications.

This may be a forerunner of things to come, as environmental crises compel society's economic sector to adopt new technological methods and recognize the need for new behavioural criteria to meet socioecological imperatives. The growing number of products being marketed as "green" and "environmentally friendly" is an example of the gradual realization that the traditional, uncritical pursuit of "growth" per se is neither ecologically sustainable nor ethically credible, especially in the eyes of those who will live in the 21st century. The prospect of common environmental disaster will accelerate the shift from the expansionist to the ecological world view (as Samuel Johnson realized in the 18th century!).

Any attempt to create a sustainable national economy will also require the restructuring of it. To this end, Canada must get away from depending on exports of its energy and raw materials, and diversify the economy through the manufacture of more value-added products. Canada's public and private sectors should collaborate in efforts to research and develop technologies appropriate to rapidly emerging national and international environmental and social imperatives. Two factors must be noted:

✦ First, a demographic and economic expansion will take place primarily in the Third World. As transnational corporations expand in these areas because of lower wages and environmental standards, they will compete increasingly successfully in North America's own bailiwick. This is a concern being voiced over NAFTA — the North American Free Trade Agreement.

✦ Second, global capital and integration of international economic systems make it increasingly difficult to set national economic policies or stringent national social and environmental standards. Indeed, critics of current free trade arrangements point to the danger of a progressive erosion of Canadian values — values that originated in the geographical uniqueness and historical legacy of the country and have created a cultural entity distinctive from that south of the border. We must recognize that, if and when Canadians shift from sustained development to sustainable development, and consequently move to implement the values and goals of an emerging ecological world view, they will be confronted with one roadblock after another by their free trade partners directly to the south, the strongest and hitherto most uncompromising champions of the expansionist paradigm.

## Toward Sustainable Forestry:
## The Case for Community Forestry

Critics of the forest industry argue that current forestry practices are not sustainable and that we require a systemic approach to forest management. For example, environmental groups, such as the Sierra Club of Western Canada, the Valhalla Society, and the Western Canada Wilderness Committee, have favoured a greater degree of community control on the basis that local groups would be more sensitive to the long-term needs of community watersheds and aware of the social and environmental benefits that can be derived from carefully managing the full spectrum of forest values. They argue that a strategy for sustainable forestry would recognize that forest ecosystems are highly complex and that each part is essential to the overall health and resilience of the forest. Consequently, all the parts must be accounted for and, in so doing, a wider range of forest values can be accommodated.

For example, forests are needed for wildlife habitats, climate regulation, recreation, and spiritual values; to maintain air and water quality; and to maintain and supply jobs and commodities. Hence, a systemic approach should allow for the protection of all the forest's functions and components. For timber extraction, a sustainable strategy would favour harvesting methods that least damage the soil and least shock the forest ecosystem. In short, such a management strategy would tend to be locally based and labour intensive.

Advocates of community forestry have argued that a sustainable forestry strategy would favour the forms of management that best approximate the forest's own natural processes. This implies the need to maintain a diversified forest stand, which, in turn, accommodates all natural successional stages and the diversity of species depending on a forest's ecosystem. With the growing uncertainty about the ability of Canada's temperate forests to withstand the effects of global climate change, they argue that it is more important than ever to maintain the natural diversity of plant and animal species to optimize the overall resilience of the ecosystem. Maintaining the overall diversity of the forest ecosystem is often cited as key to both the stability of the forest and to the stability of forest communities. Obviously, the challenge of a sustainable forestry strategy would be to create alternatives that are both environmentally and economically viable.

Undoubtedly, there will be a certain amount of economic dislocation and impact on people's lives in any move toward a sustainable approach to the management of BC's forests. Yet, there is now a growing awareness by government, forest workers, and environmentalists alike that a continuation of the status quo will result in even greater levels of social, economic, and environmental disruption.

British Columbia industry critic and professional forester Herb Hammond (1991, pp. 197–252) has proposed that forests be zoned for a variety of activities on a watershed by watershed basis. In any sustainable forestry-management plan, timber extraction would only be considered as one possible forest use and would be looked at in terms of its potential systemic effect on the future growth of trees as well as on other forest resources, such as wildlife habitats and tourism.

Hammond recommends that we move away from harsh prac-tices such as clear-cutting, slash-and-burn, pesticide use, and high grading (the removal of only the "best" timber). Where timber extraction is determined to be an acceptable use of the forest, selective logging methods would be favoured and the timber would be processed in nearby communities. Substantial parts of the forest, often entire watersheds, would be recognized for nature's intrinsic, cultural, and spiritual values. Nontimber uses, such as wilderness preservation, water supply, tourism, fish and wildlife needs, carbon sinks, and soil protection, would also be considered. The decision on how a forest should be used would be based on community and public input into the planning process and linked to a larger land-use strategy for British Columbia (Table 2).

In addition to environmental sustainability, there is a need for social and economic sustainability. According to M'Gonigle (1987):

> Community empowerment is the prerequisite to all other changes. The existing pattern of resource over-exploitation has evolved and been maintained because local communities have had virtually no control over their local resource base.

Conventional economic thinking in British Columbia has long argued the position that it is the large corporate organizations that can best meet the province's need for long-term economic stability through the efficient use of resources, based on economies of scale. Over the years, small logging companies and independent operators have been gobbled up by large companies. In fact, by 1976 almost 60 percent of the timber rights in the province were in the hands of 10 companies. By 1988, four interlinked corporate groups controlled

Table 2. Two approaches to forestry.

| Industrial Forestry | Ecoforestry |
| --- | --- |
| Trees are viewed as "products" | Forests are viewed as ecological communities |
| Short-term production goals | Long-term sustainability |
| Agricultural production model | Forest ecosystem model |
| Trees are the only cash crop | Diverse forest products |
| Tree survival dependent on humans | Self-sustaining, self-maintaining, and self-renewing |
| Chemicals | No chemicals |
| Clear-cuts | Harvesting surplus wood and selective harvesting |
| Same age stands of trees | All ages of trees |
| Monoculture of single or few species | All species of trees |
| Simplified ecosystem | Biodiversity and complexity |
| Capital intensive/corporate based | Labour intensive and locally based |
| Redesigning nature | Accepting nature's design |
| Life span, 60–100 years | Life span, millennia |
| Loss of the sacred | Sense of the sacred |

Source: Ecoforestry Institute (1993).

over 90 percent of the overall provincial cut. Moreover, a recent BC Credit Union study points out that about 70 percent of the forest industry in the province is controlled from outside of BC — of which over 40 percent is controlled from outside of Canada (Hopwood 1992, pp. 20–21).

Both the globalization of the economy and the reduction of trade barriers have enabled companies to pressure BC governments and forest employees alike to accept worker layoffs, minimal environmental standards, and a high level of annual allowable cut to remain internationally competitive (Figure 6). Given the fact that around half

Figure 6. Comparison of annual volume logged with direct forest industry jobs in British Columbia from 1961 to 1989 (source: Statistics Canada, Ministry of Forests Annual Reports).

of Canada's net balance of trade is from forest products, the political clout of the forest industry is considerable. Indeed, companies have threatened to curtail operations and relocate elsewhere unless a favourable economic climate is maintained. Recently, MacMillan Bloedel informed its workers that growing demands for old-growth preservation and pollution standards had created a situation whereby Noranda Forest Products would not be putting new investments into the Port Alberni area.

With relatively little value added to their timber, BC forest companies have been relying on the shipment of vast quantities of tree products out of the province. In the process, the long-term viability of forest communities has become increasingly precarious as the resource base is progressively eroded. Moreover, companies have been reluctant to invest directly in the diversification of local economies, preferring instead to direct surplus revenue back to the parent company and to more profitable industrialized areas, such as central Canada or the United States. In turn, competition from foreign-based companies is forcing corporations, now operating in British Columbia, to look at investment opportunities in developing countries, with their lower wage, tax, and environmental requirements.

Not surprisingly, many of British Columbia's forestry-dependent communities now feel that they are at the mercy of external corporate forces and international markets. In response, increasing numbers of people are calling for a major restructuring of current political and institutional arrangements to allow for greater local participation in the planning and management of local forest resources and for greater community control over these areas. Indeed, one definition of community forestry is "the intensive management of forest lands adjacent to municipal boundaries to best meet the social and economic requirements of people living in that community" (Lay and Phillips 1988, p. 1). Current arguments for community control include the following:

✦ Community dependence on exports of a single resource leave the local economy vulnerable to external market variations. Long-term stability requires diversification and investment in the local economy. Such development is best accomplished through local initiatives and planning.

✦ Outside control of the local resource base often results in surplus revenues being redirected elsewhere. Companies tend to be reluctant to purchase from local suppliers, invest in local manufacturing, or locate head offices and research facilities in the community. Alternatively, it is argued that a community-based forestry would more readily be able to keep revenues within the region. For example, multiple uses of the forest resource by a variety of entrepreneurial small businesses are often better able to adapt to changing markets and serve a range of specialized market requirements than are large organizations (M'Gonigle 1986, pp. 169–191). In turn, it is argued that revenues from timber could be used to offset taxes and provide funding for local social, business, and recreational projects. Wages and benefits would be more apt to stay in the community, thus providing a range of indirect benefits (Ussery 1988, pp. 14–16).

✦ Small-scale forestry can best protect the wide range of economic and environmental values. For example, community-based enterprises are more apt to be sensitive to the protection of water supplies and wildlife habitat, while providing opportunities for tourist and recreational revenue. It is argued that small-scale forestry may be less wasteful and better able to produce a wider variety of specialized wood products through intensive management. Small-scale forestry is "site-specific," using a variety of harvesting procedures and is better suited to the practice of a more environmentally sustainable "holistic" and systemically based form of management (Raphael 1981; Loomis 1990).

✦ Locally controlled resources are responsive to the changing needs, values, and life-styles of the local population. Control over one's resources gives a feeling of control over one's life. Moreover, a sense of community pride is fostered by people working together on projects in which they have helped to plan and have a long-term stake (Dunster 1989, p. 12).

Besides environmental, social, and economic sustainability, community consensus is crucial. However, it is not always easy to obtain consensus both within communities and between communities. Territoriality or "tribalism" may occur, and local governments may not reflect local community wants. Another major problem in achieving and maintaining community consensus is the lack of financial and other resources necessary to sustain protracted battles with corporate and other powerful interests.

Nevertheless, a number of coalitions have been formed involving labour, environmental, native, and business people from a variety of forestry-dependent communities. Such seemingly unexpected alliances have been in response to the frustration and inability of the provincial government to deal with resource conflicts that have become so common throughout the province.

The 1991 Bulkley Valley Community Resources Board Agreement (Bulkley Valley 1992) is representative of the kind of principles that are now being espoused by community board initiatives throughout British Columbia:

✦ The cultural, social, economic, and general well-being of people and communities should be the overriding aim of managing our natural resources.

✦ All resource activities should endeavour to be ecologically responsible and to maintain biological diversity at the landscape unit level.

✦ Development should be sustainable, enabling people of the community to maintain their quality of life without compromising the needs of future generations.

✦ Land uses in provincial forests should be balanced to optimize net benefits to the people of the district while recognizing the needs of the people of the province as a whole.

✦ There should be improved methods of assuring that the people who live in a district will have a prominent role in deciding how the resources in their district will be managed.

The Bulkley Valley Community Resources Board is made up of 12 Bulkley Valley residents who each reflect 1 or more of 16 particular resource-value perspectives. These perspectives range from "attaches particular value to timber production above other uses" and "attaches particular value to timber production by small operators" to "attaches particular value to the preservation of large tracts of wilderness, with limited access" (Bulkley Valley 1992, pp. 7–10).

Although groups such as the Bulkley Valley Community Resources Board, the Hazelton "Framework for Watershed Stewardship," the Cortes Island Forest Committee, and the Slocan Valley Watershed Alliance are a reaction to the growing frustrations over resource conflicts, they have arisen, in part, as a community response to the Brundtland Report's call for local participation and input into sustainable development strategies. The initiation of such community boards is cause for cautious optimism, as they represent a grass-roots attempt to reassert control over both lives and resources. However, the fragility of such alliances portends a shaky and uncertain future.

The goal of community sustainability is plainly laudable. Nevertheless, as described earlier, the concept of sustainable development encompasses positions with opposing views:

✦ The dominant **expansionist world view** is rooted in Enlightenment thought, in which the idea of progress through scientific and technological mastery over nature is pursued for human ends, as well as in the Gifford Pinchot model of "wise management" conservation. This position is reflected in mainstream economic theory and the belief in the ongoing growth and globalization of commodity markets; it is, in short, "sustainable economic growth."

✦ The emerging **ecological world view**, more akin to "developing environmental sustainability," is rooted in a Counter-Enlightenment and Romantic tradition that views nature and humans as a systemic web in which each of the parts is related to the larger whole and possesses intrinsic and nonutilitarian, as well as life-support and utilitarian, values. It asserts the need for limits to current forms of human and economic growth and places an emphasis on the preservation of biological diversity and wilderness areas.

In the current debates over sustainable development strategies these two positions are in stark relief. Nowhere was this more evident than in the acrimonious debates between environmentalists, International Woodworkers of America (IWA), and forest industry representatives on the Clayoquot Sound Sustainable Development Task Force. In the end, the Task Force was unable to develop a consensus-based negotiation and subsequently failed. The parties resorted to traditional value perspectives and positional bargaining: "trees versus jobs." Moreover, environmentalists felt the process was hampered from the outset by a forestry "log and talk" agenda imposed by the province (Darling 1991).

The difficulty in achieving consensual agreement often reflects the political and economic power disparities among the interested parties. Rarely is there willingness to give up one's privileged status. Perhaps it is not surprising that members of the environmental community have been so willing to endorse the concept of greater community resource control and political powers. In many respects, this stance has been a reaction to the perception that governments in British Columbia and elsewhere have mismanaged the environment and have a history of serving the economic interests of a powerful forest industry.

Historically, the Counter-Enlightenment and Romantic traditions have been the mirror image of the status quo. In reaction to the rise of large bureaucracies and political and economic centralization, its proponents have favoured various versions of decentralization and local control. In reaction to forms of universalism, it has favoured pluralism; in reaction to an industrial world's "hard" technology, it has advocated "small" or "appropriate" forms of technology. To the extent that an emerging ecological world view is still rooted in these traditional categories, its proponents will work largely in opposition to the status quo.

In the past few years, however, members of the environmental community have begun to stress the need for more effective regional environmental standards and legislation. In part, this has been a response to what is regarded as a lack of meaningful provincial forestry and environmental regulations, as well as a reaction to the opposition from members of logging communities to "outside" interference by urban environmentalists in local watersheds.

This latter point underscores an ongoing weakness in the mainstream environmentalist position. North American environmental groups may be criticized for failing to properly assess the socioeconomic and political dimensions of wilderness and resource issues and the extent to which environmental degradation is predicated largely on existing political and economic structures (Thrupp 1989). Environmentalists are easy targets for criticism from local people who feel out of control and marginalized, whether they are from Ucluelet on Vancouver Island or the developing nations of the South. Without a proper critique of existing socioeconomic structures and of potential viable alternatives for the members of resource-dependent communities, the environmental movement will remain an easy target for those whose interests have been tied to the status quo.

Indeed, the rise of antienvironmentalist "community" coalitions under the banner of "share" or "wise-use" groups underscores how the environmental position can be seen as opposing the public's need for economic and social stability (Emery 1991). Environmental issues were high on the list of public concerns during the late 1980s and early 1990s until a Canadian recession brought economic and employment issues to the fore. Again, as the 1993 federal election illustrated, voters' concern over the need to get out of the recession and increase jobs took precedence over previously voiced concerns about the environment. This gave a strong impression that Canadians are inadequately informed about environmental protection and that enhancement is both "good economics" and "good business" for their communities and themselves.

What has often been ignored by governmental, business, and environmental organizations is how central social justice and equity issues are in the Brundtland Report's interpretation of strategies for sustainable development. For example, the report states (WCED 1987, pp. 38, 43):

> Physical sustainability cannot be secured unless development policies pay attention to such considerations as changes in access to resources and in the distribution of costs and benefits. Even the narrow notion of physical sustainability implies a concern for

*social equity between generations, a concern that must logically be extended to equity within each generation.*

*New approaches must involve programs of social development, particularly to improve the position of women in society, to protect vulnerable groups, and to promote local participation in decision making.*

Recently, these concerns over the future of BC communities were recognized by the British Columbia Round Table on the Environment and Economy (1991, p. 7):

*Achieving social equity, and therefore social sustainability, means having access to: the decision-making processes affecting the sustainable community; equal opportunities for education and training; adequate recreational opportunities, health care, social support services, and housing; a quality of environment; and an opportunity to earn a livelihood.*

Such statements underscore a growing recognition that environmental, socioeconomic, and political dimensions must all be recognized in discussions on community survival, and that matters of human well-being must be accounted for in strategies for environmental protection (Prince 1992). It also raises the question of how current trends toward global liberal trade policies and a North American economic market fly in the face of the ability of resource communities to maintain themselves.

Such concerns were addressed at the first Tin Wis Conference, south of Tofino in 1989, and again at Port Alberni in 1990. The Tin Wis Coalition is an umbrella organization for forest labour members, environmentalists, business people, and native people. Perhaps what is significant in its position is a belief that any meaningful goal of environmental sustainability must be directly linked to an analysis of current corporate control and political and economic decision-making. As Cholette (1992, p. 12) notes:

*While the coalition has been sympathetic to those who work to immediately stop environmental destruction, the focus of Tin Wis and other similar groups has been not to act to protect various aspects of the environment, but to take part in the ecological project of creating fundamental cultural, economic, and political change that will sustain the natural world.*

## Defining Sustainable Agriculture

The federal Department of Agriculture and its provincial counterparts have recently offered a working definition of sustainable agriculture (Canada 1991, p. 9):

> *Sustainable agri-food systems are those that are economically viable, and meet society's need for safe and nutritious food, while conserving and enhancing Canada's natural resources and the quality of the environment for future generations.*

The report *Sustainable Agriculture: The Research Challenge* (Science Council of Canada 1992, pp. 15–16) suggests that implicit in this definition are the following principles of sustainable agriculture and food production:

✦ Thorough integration of the farming system with natural processes;

✦ Reduction of those inputs most likely to harm the environment;

✦ Greater use of the biological and genetic potential of plant and animal species;

✦ Improvement in the match between cropping patterns and land resources to ensure the sustainability of current agricultural production levels;

✦ Efficient production, with an emphasis on improved farm management and conservation of soil, water, energy, and biological resources; and

✦ Development of food processing, packaging, distribution, and consumption practices consistent with sound environmental management.

Similarly, Dover and Talbot (1987, p. 63) list nine conditions necessary for a sustainable agricultural system:

✦ Replenishment of soil nutrients removed by crops;

✦ Maintenance of the soil's physical condition;

✦ Constant or increasing humus levels in the soil;

✦ No buildup of weeds, pests, or diseases;

✦ No increase in soil acidity or toxic elements;

✦ Control of soil erosion;

✦ Minimization of off-farm contamination of the environment;

✦ Maintenance of adequate habitat for wildlife; and

✦ Conservation of genetic resources.

These points clearly show that sustainable agriculture is much more than a set of techniques and practices. It is a philosophy that views agricultural communities and economies as subsystems of the ecological systems on which they depend. For example, the goals of such agriculture are fundamentally different from those of conventional practices, as it attempts to achieve "long-term yield stability with minimal environmental impact — in contrast to focusing more on short-term goals, such as maximum yields" (Stinner and Blair 1990, p. 138).

Sustainable agriculture also attempts to improve the quality of the food produced, as well as the social and economic conditions of farm and rural communities (Parr et al. 1990, pp. 50–67). In this respect, critics of conventional agriculture argue that long-term community viability should involve participation in decisions concerning the rural community. Similar arguments are also being made for the long-term stability of forest-based communities.

Like sustainable forestry, sustainable agriculture is the application of systems thinking: agriculture must be regarded as more than the sum of its parts. It is a complex system, defined by the interrelationships and interactions within it (Edwards 1990, pp. 249–264). The farm cannot be properly understood apart from the larger social community, food production, and economic systems, and the ecological systems of which it is a component.

A systemic approach to agriculture focuses on the relationships and processes within a system, as well as on the flow and cycles of energy and matter. Thus, a systems approach to the design of agriculture looks at interactions among the various components and processes, as opposed to the conventional approach, which tends to focus on maximizing one aspect, such as production or yields.

All systems are characterized by processes of self-maintenance or negative-feedback loops. In a natural ecosystem, insects that can be pests in an agroecosystem are kept in check by predators and parasites. Such negative-feedback processes must be incorporated into the design of agroecosystems to promote overall stability and resilience.

The ecological system of the farm should be managed in terms of its biological relationships: the beneficial being encouraged, disruption being minimized. The principal characteristics of natural ecosystems should be integrated into the agroecosystem, such as complexity, nutrient cycling, and the sun as the system's principal energy source. The farmer's main task is to balance the need for high yields from a few systemic components with that of the long-term stability of the system as a whole. Naturally, the ability of a farmer or manager to play such a role "depends on a thorough understanding of the processes governing soil chemistry and biology, plant nutrition, and the forces that keep insects, pathogens, and weeds in check" (Dover and Talbot 1987, p. 6).

Table 3 illustrates how dramatically the ecological systems approach contrasts with the conventional, industrial agricultural model. Although conventional farming can obtain high yields by using large quantities of chemical and energy outputs, it has done so at an increasing cost to the long-term viability of the ecosystem and to the stability of farming communities.

Maintaining a healthy agricultural environment goes hand in hand with maintaining viable farm communities. A sustainable

Table 3. Two approaches to farming.

| Industrial–Agricultural Model | Ecological, Systems Approach |
| --- | --- |
| Primarily concerned with flows of matter and money through the system | Concerned also with the cycles of energy and matter |
| Focused on productivity (output of labour or land) | Also considers production functions and maintenance |
| Evaluation of system done in terms of economic efficiency (output per unit of capital input) | Also assesses nutrient cycling rates, stability, and energy efficiency |
| Relies heavily on a large capital investment and extensive infrastructure | Relies on a deep understanding of the ecological processes of the agroecosystem |

Source: Dover and Talbot (1987).

agricultural system must be able to generate sufficient income for primary producers to ensure the stability and health of the farm communities. Or, as one critic of agribusiness suggests, a sustainable agricultural system "requires the regeneration and maintenance of the agricultural community, which rests on tradition, and the support and commitment of generations of farmers" (Drengson 1986, p. 134).

## Assessment and Recommendations

Growing farm debts; the need for agricultural support from federal and provincial governments; a declining farming population (Figure 7); foreign subsidies and food wars; the loss of soil productivity; the loss of prime agricultural land to development and erosion; and the increasing reliance on fertilizer, biotechnology, and chemical inputs all point to a growing crisis in Canadian agriculture. In much the same way that Canadian forestry has focused on an industrial model and tended to ignore the maintenance of ecological processes, so too the trend in Canadian agriculture has been based on economies of scale, with increasing levels of environmental damage. Farming

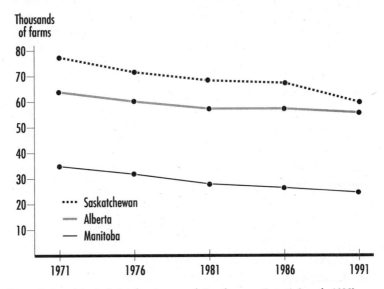

Figure 7. Canada's declining farming population (source: Census Canada 1992).

communities, like forest-based communities, have witnessed increasing financial difficulties and the progressive loss of community members.

In a 1986 study for Agriculture Canada, Paul Robinson (1986, pp. 6–7) identified 35 different governmental hindrances. The primary hindrance was the policy to ignore sustainable agriculture and emphasize the use of agricultural chemicals. Robinson's data revealed that many farmers believe that there is an explicit policy at all levels of government to ignore sustainable agriculture.

The second major hindrance was allowing the agricultural chemical industry to exert excessive influence on the government. Again, many farmers felt that departments of agriculture work too closely with the chemical companies. Agricultural ministries promote the use of chemicals and strangle efforts to examine alternatives. Conventional agricultural thinking often starts by assuming that chemicals are the cure.

Many of the concepts of sustainable agriculture challenge conventional agriculture thinking. Some concepts may even transcend current scientific theory. Government extension agents, researchers, and agencies are poorly informed about sustainable agriculture. To properly assess sustainable agriculture, federal and provincial departments of agriculture must become better informed and be supportive of sustainable agriculture initiatives.

More than ever, there is the need to develop policies that take a systemic approach and integrate the socioeconomic needs of communities with the biophysical needs of the land. There is a need for greater community participation in the policies that affect rural life. Nutrient cycles and the integrity and resiliency of ecological systems must be maintained. Conventional agricultural practices must move away from monocultures. Research should be initiated into polycultures and small-scale farming. Farming techniques based on a diversity of species, although more labour intensive, are more productive in terms of total plant yield and tend to be less dependent on fertilizers, herbicides, and expensive forms of machinery. Biological and alternative controls for pests and diseases should also be investigated.

Sustainable agriculture depends on the preservation of prime agricultural lands. The country cannot afford to leave land use to the "free market." Yet municipalities all too frequently ignore the need to preserve land. Unfortunately, a jurisdictional gridlock often favours tarmac over soil. Consequently, a high level of support must be given to the idea of agricultural land reserves — especially land that is close to urban centres, such as BC's Fraser Valley and Ontario's Niagara Escarpment region.

Tax credits and other financial incentives should help farmers raise organic produce. The organic food industry is quickly gaining public support as concern about the environment and human health grows (Tisdall 1992).

Finally, sustainable agriculture is motivated by long-term goals and objectives, as exemplified by the principle of stewardship of the land for future generations. A sustainable food system must be based on something other than short-term financial planning.

*Chapter 8*

# Canada as an Organic Society

*A*s *we near the third millennium, an increasingly inter-dependent world is at a critical watershed. Never before have we humans as a species, and as individual men and women, had such an opportunity to shape our common future.*

— DeFries and Malone (1989, p. v)

To encourage Canadian economic sustainability, decision-making and production should take place at the regional and community levels. Of paramount importance is the need to maintain food security in Canada into the future. As with community forest boards, this makes sense because it leads to more sensitized management of Canada's resources and a more diversified and self-reliant economy. Given the history and size of Canada, there is always the question of at what level are decisions made.

How does one resolve the fundamental dilemma between large-scale organization, rationalization, coordination, and national planning on the one hand, and localism, community control, diversity, responsiveness, and grass-roots participation on the other? It is appropriate to quote the views of the Canadian political philosopher J.A. Corry (1981, pp. 233–234):

> *The large bureaucracies of central government now exert a sustained and persuasive influence on legislatures and cabinets and have blinkers which focus their vision on the amplifying of their administrative reach. The first requirement for a turn-around is an aroused public opinion which warns political parties that legitimacy as well as adequate powers is at stake. Democracy must be seen as capable of redeeming its earlier promise that the people*

*can shape important features of their own destiny. If the current*
*spreading belief that they are being managed and manipulated*
*cannot be overcome, the faith in democracy will fail. An inspiring*
*faith will be succeeded by naked force.*

According to Corry, the desire of provinces and regions for less
centralization and more opportunity to manage their own affairs is
based on the argument that governments closer to home will be
more visible and responsive to people's needs. He contends that we
should be looking for ways to assure grass-roots organizations that
they can reassert a larger measure of control over matters that affect
them intimately at the local and regional levels.

Charles Taylor, of McGill University, has advocated "communi-
tarianism" as a means for communities and minority groups to use
political avenues to defend collective cultural values and goals. He
distinguishes this from the American adherence to "procedural
liberalism," whereby "individual rights must always come first, and,
along with nondiscrimination provisions, must take precedence over
collective goals" (Taylor 1992, p. 56).

Taylor describes the Meech Lake debate as a contest between
Canadians who believed in the fundamental universality of individual rights, as reflected in the Canadian Charter of Rights and
Freedoms, and those who believed that, in certain cases (as in the
proposed granting of distinct society status to Quebec), collective
rights should also be recognized. Indeed, it has been argued that the
adoption of the Canadian Charter has greatly accelerated Canada's
integration into American political culture. Consequently, the granting of special status to Quebec or to native groups in the form
of self-government was interpreted by many English-speaking
Canadians as a rejection of the universality of this model, to the
extent that it is entrenched by the Charter. On the other hand, as
Taylor (1992, p. 60) notes:

*Quebec saw that the move to give the Charter precedence imposed*
*a form of liberal society that was alien to it, and to which Quebec*
*could never accommodate itself without surrendering its identity.*

Taylor (1977, p. 67) believes that Canada's division into provinces, in most cases, represents an important sociological reality, embodying distinct histories and cultures.

> *It is realistic to see these as units of autonomous planning —*
> *indeed, it would be very unrealistic to see our future any other way;*
> *Canada is an uncentralizable country.... Ultimately, it would be a*
> *healthy thing if our regions evolved away from the homogenization*
> *of their ways of life which has been steadily going ahead in the past*
> *decades.*

Although one may agree with the overall thrust of Corry's and Taylor's arguments, it is useful to conceive of the centralization–decentralization issue not solely in terms of a simple dichotomy. For, as Charles Taylor points out, a major question will have to be answered: Can decentralization be combined with a common purpose?

The Canadian constitutional debates have exemplified this dichotomous way of thinking. Canadians were asked to choose between the universality of individual rights and the protection of cultural minorities; between a Canada that is centralized in its fundamental powers and one that is decentralized. To accept this two-valued approach leads us into a dichotomous trap. As Canadians, we are often asked to make a choice between our communities. Because we belong to a number of communities — municipal, provincial, regional, national, ethnic, and international — Canadians require not the traditional two-valued approach, but a multirelational or systemic approach.

First, all Canadian communities can be recognized as integral systemic components of Canadian society, so that discrimination against any one of them adversely affects all the others. Second, movement within this societal system can no longer be perceived as unidirectional. An initiative may originate in any one of our communities, and its impact on the others will result in a return of further impacts — feedbacks — to the originating source.

What does this mean for the centralization–decentralization issue that continues to bedevil Canadian politics? We should not have to make a choice between centralized powers and our requirements

for localism, grass-roots participation, and diversity. We can acknowledge and support diversity as long as there are adequate
safeguards for fundamental rights. In turn, we can favour both
centralization and decentralization concurrently, with feedback
loops proceeding in both directions at once. Canadian society
comprises a number of communities — "a community of communities" — and each can be mandated to perform specific functions.

From a systems perspective, it may be argued that the more
geopolitically comprehensive a given level of government, the more
comprehensive, in turn, must be its planning. For example, the
federal government needs to be provided with the means to engage
in activities encompassing national standards for the protection of
the environment and human rights, as well as the taxation and
disbursement of revenues on an equitable, nationwide basis. Hence,
we can accept the logic of entrusting to the federal government
jurisdiction over areas such as national defence, the protection of
Arctic space and resources, and the redistribution of financial
resources by means of such devices as equalization transfers and
social welfare programs. Conversely, the more restricted the geopolitical jurisdiction of our Canadian communities, the proportionately
greater opportunity for local initiatives, grass-roots participation, and
functional diversity in the planning and use of resources.

In terms of systems thinking, a whole is more than the sum of
its parts. Indeed it is more, because any system — whether an
old-growth temperate rain forest or a nation-state — is not merely
the simple addition of its separate parts but also the product of their
constitutive relations and consequent interactions.

So it is with Canada. It is at once the totality of its biophysical
systems and of its human communities, as well as everything these
relationships create. Pierre Trudeau once asked: "Who speaks for
Canada?" It is these same individuals who also speak for Prince
Edward Island and Quebec, for Winnipeg and Whitehorse. Charles
Taylor (1977, pp. 67–70) contends that we do have the environmental and societal potential to create "a sense of Canadian identity
and purpose." However, to achieve them, citizens at all levels of

community should be engaging in an ongoing dialogue about shared problems together with their societal options and future goals.

## Sustaining Our Goals

The United States will always be a dominant factor in Canada's geographic location and trade pattern. However, this does not mean that Canada must inevitably move toward continental integration and absorption into the United States. If Canadians reject continentalism, is their only recourse some kind of protectionist–isolationist stance? Given the extent of Canada's dependence on foreign trade, this cannot be a credible strategy. When Canadians shift their perspective from the South–North axis and recognize the economic and political significance of Europe and the Pacific, they can escape the potential problems associated with being tied too closely with a North American trading bloc. Canada might do better to engage in global economic and political strategies.

Because of a deteriorating environment, Canada should reassess its policy for its resource sectors, together with a new economic–environmental strategy to revise the "hewers of wood, drawers of water" syndrome. The new Clinton administration in Washington is faced with a US economy that is a declining force in the global marketplace. Consequently, Canadians should reconsider their ties to a weakening American capitalist empire.

The South, where the majority of the world's population lives, is becoming increasingly political and emancipated from economic colonialism. Canada should look to this emerging global socioeconomic–environmental order to rebuild its own "made-in-Canada" economy. Such a strategy would be informed by principles of national and international social, economic, and environmental sustainability, gearing trade and development policies to stringent environmental standards and human rights. In this way, Canada can adopt as a national goal the Parti Québecois slogan — *Maitres chez nous* (masters in our own house) — in the sphere of political economy and, in so doing, strengthen its own sense of national identity.

Bernard Shaw once quipped that the British and the Americans are divided by a common language. Each nationality feels secure in its own historical roots, values, and life-styles. Each is easily recognizable by the rest of the world. Yet, perhaps with the exception of Quebec, Canada is growing to be increasingly like its southern neighbour. This tendency, of great concern to pro-Canada groups such as the Council for Canadians, is largely due to modern technology, which integrates aspects of Canadian and American culture and blurs the international boundary. This is exemplified by the new CP Rail logo, which merges visually the Canadian and American flags.

If Canada is to survive as a unique member of the global community with a character readily identifiable to both itself and the world at large, it will not come from either imitating or, conversely, rejecting American values and behaviour. Survival will depend on the extent to which Canadian society finds the courage, vision, and initiative to play its own constructive role in the new sociopolitical and environmental situation in the 21st century.

To play such a constructive role, Canadians should re-evaluate who they are and the basic principles of Canadian society. There are two possible scenarios for our future: the worst and the best possible.

The first scenario takes its title from George Grant's *Lament for a Nation*. It follows the perspective of Jacques Ellul, the prominent French critic of technological values, who holds that technology is now the dominant homogenizing force and is inextricably tied to industrial capitalism and liberalism, all of which tend to be equated with "progress." Given that science and technology tend to universalize, modern civilization makes all local cultures anachronistic.

Applying this argument to Canada, our culture floundered on the age of progress. The argument that Canada, as a local culture, must disappear can, therefore, be stated in three steps (Grant 1980, p. 54):

✦ First, people move ineluctably toward membership in the universal and homogeneous state.

✦ Second, Canadians live next to a society that is the heart of modernity.

✦   Third, nearly all Canadians think that modernity is good, so
nothing essentially distinguishes Canadians from Americans.

In turn, Grant (1980, p. 65) argues:

*The founders of the US took their thought from the 18th century
Enlightenment. Their rallying cry was "freedom." There was no
place in their cry for the organic conservatism that pre-dated the
age of progress. Their "right-wing" and "left-wing" are just different
species of liberalism.*

This liberalism is tied historically to technology and "progress," with
the latter's insistence on "efficiency" and standardization. The liberal
tradition in Canada has subscribed, in turn, to laissez-faire capitalism,
individualism, a belief in the land as a resource to be exploited for
human "progress," and "continentalism," or the ideal of seeing
Canada as part of a larger North American industrial empire. This
has been the view from Laurier to Goldwin Smith and Mackenzie
King; to this group should now be added such neoconservatives as
Brian Mulroney.

Classical liberalism has always been cosmopolitan, a major
Enlightenment principle functioning at the expense of particular and
local loyalties. It is the celebration of reason over emotion, of human
freedom from restraints, and of society's individual members. Given
the technocratic values of "efficiency" and "economies of scale,"
liberalism lends itself to the centralization of power by large bureaucracies and large centralized governments. Taken all together, these
principles and behavioural dynamics made Grant doubt whether
Canada — a pluralistic and multicultural society — could withstand
the forces of Americanization and cultural assimilation. In short, this
has resulted in the ongoing co-optation of Canada by values of the
Enlightenment and expansionist world view.

However, perhaps the best possible scenario for this country is
based on its own cultural antecedents, summarized in Grant's (1980)
term "organic conservatism." Grant views an organic society as one
based on the principle of mutual obligations. Recognition of the
diversity and varying potentials of different peoples is balanced by
recognition of their equal worth. Because the organic society is based
on mutual obligations among all groups and classes, it embraces the

principles of social justice and equity — two fundamental principles of sustainable development. Such a society is perceived to be rooted in organic. change and natural growth. Three key notions are tolerance, civility, and compromise.

Traditionally, Canadian organic conservatism rejects the homogeneous state, and is suspicious of "progress" equated with consumerism. Neither does it deem all technologies good. There is always the need to foster quality of life, even if this means opposing the conformist, dehumanizing forces of the liberal technological state in order to celebrate the diversity of regions and human existence. Nationalism is rejected when interpreted as "we-versus-them"; it is rooted in patriotism, a love of the land, and a sense of place. Only with a proud respect for one's own roots and community can another culture and home be fully appreciated (Taylor 1926). The ideals of this tradition are linked to a conservative–conservation ethic that recognizes the need to balance societal change with ecological continuity and maintain a viable equilibrium between the needs of the community and those of the natural.

Canadians like to think of themselves as possessing a sense of community and order, and a respect for human rights and human diversity. Indeed, many Canadian institutions and social programs reflect a conservative–radical mix that makes them unique on this continent. Northrop Frye points out that because Canadians fought their wars of independence against the United States, it is logical that the collective Canadian psyche should harbour a strong suspicion of the mercantilist Whiggery that won the American Revolution and, in turn, evolved into the contemporary forces of classical liberal and neoconservative ideology. "The Canadian point of view is at once more conservative and more radical than Whiggery, closer to the aristocracy and to democracy than to oligarchy" (Frye quoted in Taylor 1982, p. 213).

For too long, Canadians have tended to react to foreign initiatives. They should move to a proactive stance with the two interrelated strategies of environmental and societal concerns. Canadians are blessed with physical resources; but ecological problems must be remedied. Canadians have the potential to restore and protect their environment, if they begin to act now. They have the societal resources as well; but do they have the essential political will and steadfastness?

As the Brundtland Report shows, the countries of the world will increasingly have to recognize that economic and social sectors must be related to the natural world. In short, the contemporary expansionist world view of unbridled expansionism and exploitation will have to come to terms with critical, and often irreversible, environmental concerns. Canada needs to free itself now from the environmentally unsustainable consequences of a neoconservative economic agenda and the ongoing colonialism of transnational corporations.

Canadians have traditions that are inherent in an "organic" society. It may be argued that they are better equipped to move toward such a goal than their friends to the south, whose culture is so deeply rooted in Lockean and Enlightenment values.

## The Need for Committed Action

The implications of a growing environmental awareness and concern for the ecology of the planet have been likened in their importance to a second Copernican revolution. Whereas the heliocentric theory of the Copernican revolution removed the Earth from the centre of the universe, so too is the current environmental revolution a growing recognition that humanity is no longer the centre of the biosphere, but a highly dependent and inextricably related subsystem (Hall and Hanson 1992, p. 11). Traditional notions of security rooted in the Westphalian logic of the nation-state system must be completely reassessed in light of the imperatives of our planetary ecology. Consequently, conventional discussions in the traditional Western ideology of domination and control over both nature and territorial states must be abandoned. We need approaches that favour consensus and cooperation (Dalby 1992, pp. 117–119). The sustainability of the planetary ecology requires an immediate effort to reformulate existing international economic arrangements and address issues dealing with the redistribution of wealth. This raises the question of the appropriateness of contemporary Western capitalist adherence to marketplace economics and the values of consumerism.

During the 1980s, Canada's traditional "organic conservative" or "Tory" values gradually disintegrated in favour of a liberal, neo-conservative agenda. Canada's political and economic makeup has taken on many of the attributes of its neighbour to the south: the recognition of the sanctity of individual rights and a commitment to a belief in the virtues of marketplace economics as a major force in determining the structures and organization of society. Ironically, at the very time that many Canadians are rediscovering their political and cultural traditions and are moving toward a conserver society, policymakers are moving in the opposite direction.

In the late 1980s and early 1990s, opinion polls showed that Canadians were very concerned about the state of the environment. The federal government responded to the findings of the Brundtland Report of 1987 by hosting a number of major global environmental conferences, including the 1987 forum that resulted in the Montreal Protocol on Substances that Deplete the Ozone Layer and the 1989 Toronto Conference on the Changing Atmosphere. The federal government's National Task Force report initiated national, provincial, and territorial roundtables to develop strategies for sustainable development.

In the late 1980s, environmental rhetoric was everywhere. By the early 1990s, the political will and the economic resources needed to carry through economic policies with environmental sustainability were quickly fading. In part, the problem was ideological. Despite the rhetoric about sustainable development and the idea that a healthy economy requires a healthy environment, the federal government was deeply committed to the tenets of an expansionist economy. With the Canadian economy in the midst of a recession, polls began to show that Canadians were concerned more about their pocketbooks than about the state of nature. Nowhere is this rapid reversal in commitment to environmental action witnessed more than in the tabling of Canada's Green Plan.

In the Green Plan's first document for public discussion — *A Framework for Discussion on the Environment* — Environment Minister Lucien Bouchard (1990) had written that the government of Canada was determined "to make Canada, by the year 2000, the industrial world's most environmentally friendly country." Yet, with the release of the final document, and a new environment minister, this statement had been removed. In turn, the Green Plan was being quickly criticized by environmentalists as having too little in the way of funding and political clout to carry through on its goal of setting Canada on the road to sustainability.

As Arthur Hanson — an international authority on environmental issues and President and CEO of the International Institute for Sustainable Development in Winnipeg — has noted, the $3 billion (CA) given to the Green Plan over a 5-year period must be compared to the federal government's ongoing commitment to such projects as the decision to buy $4.4 billion worth of antisubmarine EH-101 helicopters and its decision to keep putting billions of dollars into Hibernia offshore oil (Hall and Hanson 1992, p. 306). (The Chrétien government cancelled the helicopter program but is still committed to Hibernia.) Neither federal nor provincial governments have put much research money into such areas as alternative forestry techniques, organic agriculture, or renewable energy sources. Indeed, the Quebec government continues to support the $13 billion Great Whale Hydro Quebec project, even though it has been criticized as a potential environmental disaster and a cultural disaster for the Cree Indians of that region.

## The Earth Summit

The Brundtland Report stimulated the United Nations to mount another global conference. This United Nations Conference on Environment and Development (UNCED) was held in Rio de Janeiro, from the 3rd to the 14th of June 1992, on the 20th anniversary of the Stockholm environmental conference. UNCED became known as the Earth Summit because it brought together the largest number of world leaders in history.

In opening the Earth Summit, Maurice Strong, who had also headed up the Stockholm conference, noted that in the 20 years from 1972 to 1992, global population had increased by 1.7 billion people — a number almost equivalent to the world's total population at the beginning of the 20th century. Of this 1.7 billion people, 1.5 billion were in the developing nations of the South, the countries least able to support them. In that same 20-year period, world GNP had increased by $20 trillion (US), with only 15 percent of this increase accruing to the South. Such a growth model, with its accompanying patterns of production and consumption, "is not sustainable for the rich; nor can it be replicated by the poor. To continue along this pathway could lead to the end of our civilization" (Strong 1992).

Public expectations before the conference had been high, and for 12 days the rhetoric and negotiations were continuous (Roche 1993). The Earth Summit produced five documents:

✦ **Biodiversity Convention** — This is a legally binding treaty that requires inventories of plants and wildlife, and plans to protect endangered species. Signatories must share research, profits, and technology with nations whose genetic resources they use. With then Prime Minister Brian Mulroney, Canada was given high praise for being the first government to sign and subsequently ratify the Convention. In contrast, then US President George Bush refused to sign because, although he agreed with its objectives, he believed that the Convention threatened the protection of patents and intellectual property rights. Later, however, President Clinton did sign the Convention.

✦ **Convention on Global Warming** — Signed by 154 nations, this legally binding treaty calls for a global commitment to reduce carbon dioxide emissions by the year 2000 to levels lower than those of 1990. Signatories are required to prepare progress reports detailing their actions to cut greenhouse gases, and these will be reviewed by a special committee that could later modify the treaty to establish specific emission levels and target dates (an eventuality that the European nations are already promoting).

✦ **Statement on Forest Principles** — A nonbinding agreement, adopted by consensus, it fell short of original plans to make it a binding convention.

✦ **Declaration on Environment and Development** — Also known as the "Rio Declaration," it recommends a number of legal principles for achieving sustainable development, such as public access to government information on the environment and calling on nations to use environmental-impact statements and to exercise caution in their development plans. Again, the Declaration provides a basis for structural change by maintaining that eradicating poverty is an "indispensable requirement" for sustainable development. It emphasizes the special responsibility of developed countries to achieve global environmental restoration because of their technological and financial capabilities, and their consumptive capacities and pollution production.

✦ **Agenda 21** — Described as the most comprehensive document to emerge from the Earth Summit, this massive work calls for national action and international cooperation to achieve sustainable development. Its 39 chapters of nonbinding recommendations serve as a blueprint for action into the next century and cover virtually all areas affecting the relationship between the environment and the economy.

The Earth Summit also came in for sharp criticism, mainly for sins of omission:

✦ In the **Biodiversity Convention**, no deadlines are set for implementing its provisions. Again, because of the original American objections, the language of the treaty is relatively weak.

✦ Even though the **Convention on Global Warming** is a binding treaty that aims to curb emissions of carbon dioxide, methane, and other greenhouse gases, the Convention does not commit any nation to hold the gases at particular levels. The European nations wanted such a commitment, but the United States was opposed and forced a compromise position. "Although the climate convention is an important first step, it will only slow the rate of climate change because greenhouse gas emissions already exceed the Earth's carrying capacity. Further cuts are needed" (Chiras 1994, p. 562).

✦ As for the **Statement on Forest Principles**, this document fell far short of original plans because of North–South differences. The developed countries proposed an agreement that would help preserve tropical rain forests; the developing countries wanted to include forests in the temperate and boreal latitudes. As outlined by Roche (1993, p. 93):

> *Except for finances, no issue proved so divisive. The North sees tropical rain forests as a treasure trove of biodiversity and greenhouse gas sinks that absorb carbon dioxide and thus keep global warming in check. For the South, the forests are resources ripe for exploration (as occurred in the North) as potential farmland and a free source of fuel. India and Malaysia particularly refused any binding commitment to preserve forests. When the North refused to accompany its admonitions with money, the South dug in.*
>
> *The result has been described as "a set of principles that underscores sovereign rights of nations to exploit their forests, legitimizing existing policies in those countries that are currently endangering the world's forests" (Chiras 1994, p. 563).*

✦ Conceived as an "Earth Charter" that would bind nations to principles on which to build a new global partnership, the **Declaration on Environment and Development** was watered down during the preparatory meetings. The North refused to concede the South's right to develop because this would have opened the door to legal demands for financial assistance. The resulting nonbinding set of principles makes up a declaration that, while making a useful start on global problems, has been described as "mushy and ambiguous" (Principle 24, for example, states: "Warfare is inherently destructive of sustainable development....").

✦ Despite important recommendations, **Agenda 21** is nonbinding and has other serious weaknesses. A commitment by developed nations to donate a certain percentage of their annual GNP was eliminated. Agenda 21 proposes no new ways of eliminating debt or of accelerating the transition to sustainable energy systems because of pressure from Kuwait, Saudi Arabia, and the

United States. All references to full-cost pricing were eliminated, and the chapter on forestry has no recommended policy of sustainable forest management. Perhaps the most serious deficiency is found in the chapter on population, which "fails to underscore the importance of population control to sustainable development and avoids the term family planning altogether, reportedly because of pressure from the Vatican" (Chiras 1994, p. 563).

The Earth Summit, critics aver, could not be called very successful, although it was by no means a failure. To use the analogy of the curate's egg, it was "good in parts." But as Douglas Roche (1993, pp. 93–94) points out, it began a new process of planetary management:

> The Earth Summit succeeded in putting environment and development in the same category that military priorities used to occupy alone. It also elevated understanding beyond single issue solutions, as if money by itself, or population control by itself, could solve the environmental crisis.... That it did not achieve the response demanded by the gravity of the issues is not a mark against the Earth Summit but reveals the work still to be done in overcoming financial and political self-interest before a new world order can take shape.

In short, what the peoples of the world must henceforth instruct their governments to do is translate Rio's theory and principles into action — rhetoric into results.

In the past decade, Canada has put its signature to a number of international environmental documents. Unfortunately, action at the international level has often been frustrated at the national level of implementation and enforcement. It may be argued that Canada could be well on its way to becoming "the industrial world's most environmentally friendly country" if it were to ratify and implement, at home, the policies that it has signed internationally. Indeed, the environmental principles already set forth in various international conventions, if acted upon, would go a long way toward implementing those points that have already been stated earlier about criteria for sustainable development. Table 4, which takes a cursory look at some of these agreements, illustrates this point.

Table 4. Selected principles from international conventions to which
Canada is a signatory.

### World Charter of Nature (1982)

Activities which are likely to pose a significant risk to nature shall be preceded by an exhaustive examination; their proponents shall demonstrate that expected benefits outweigh potential damage to nature, and where potential adverse effects are not fully understood, the activities should not proceed (11.b). Activities which are likely to cause irreversible damage to nature shall be avoided (11.a).

All areas of the earth, both land and sea, shall be subject to these principles of conservation; special protection shall be given to unique areas, to representative samples of all the different types of ecosystems and to the habitats of rare or endangered species (3).

Every form of life is unique, warranting respect regardless of its worth to [humans], and to accord other organisms such recognition, [humans] must be guided by a moral code of action (a).

Knowledge of nature shall be broadly disseminated by all possible means, particularly by ecological education as an integral part of general education (20).

### Agenda 21 (1992)

The growth of world population and production combined with unsustainable consumption patterns places increasingly severe stress on the life-supporting capacities of our planet (5.2). Unsustainable patterns of production and consumption are increasing the quantities and variety of environmentally persistent wastes at unprecedented rates (21.7).

Forests worldwide have been and are being threatened by uncontrolled degradation and conversion to other types of land uses...and environmentally harmful mismanagement including...unsustainable commercial logging...and the impacts of loss and degradation of forests are in the form of soil erosion, loss of biological diversity, damage to wildlife habitats and degradation of watershed areas (11.12).

Many of the problems have arisen from a development model that is environmentally destructive and from a lack of protection (18.45). Conserve their biodiversity and use their biological resources sustainably, and to ensure that activities within their jurisdiction or control do not cause damage to the biological diversity of other states or of areas beyond the limits of national jurisdiction (15.3).

Environmentally sound waste management must go beyond the mere safe disposal or recovery of wastes that are generated and seek to address the root cause of the problem by attempting to change unsustainable patterns of production and consumption (17.23). Effective prevention requires action through effective monitoring and the enforcement and imposition of appropriate penalties (20.20). Equitable implementation of the polluter pays principle (20.39).

### Rio Declaration (1992)

In order to protect the environment, the precautionary approach shall be widely applied by States according to their capabilities. Where there are threats of serious irreversible damage, lack of full scientific certainty shall not be used as a reason for postponing cost-effective measures or preventing environmental degradation (Principle 15).

## The Challenge for New Canadian Initiatives

Canada has come to a fork in the road or a "bifurcation point." In terms of systems theory, this refers to a period of extreme crisis when the existing system can no longer remain stable. Consequently, the system either collapses into its component parts or reorganizes to a new level of systemic integration and dynamic equilibrium with its larger environment. The same arguments used to describe the forestry and agricultural sectors can be used to describe Canada's energy sector. Significant financial resources have to be targeted to encourage and develop much-needed alternative energy programs. The longer we delay, the more options are lost.

Systems use negative-feedback mechanisms to reduce disturbances, maintain their existing structures, and prevent overdue reorganization, transformation, and change. This can be seen in British Columbia's current forestry policies.

Resource depletion, political and constitutional uncertainty (including Quebec and Western alienation, and aboriginal and minority claims), a growing domestic economic crisis, and the rapidly changing international political, economic, and environmental imperatives are causing disruptions. To obtain societal, economic, and environmental sustainability, major structural changes are needed. Canada's prosperity has been gained at the expense of degrading its natural resources, and this will have to change. Canadians will be faced with a decision either to allow the political and economic collapse of their country or to see and use this fork in the road as an opportunity to try a new social and ecological agenda.

Canadian society and the environment have collided, and immediate remedies and actions are needed. Change can only begin, however, when it is acknowledged that the social and economic institutions are subsystems of the larger Canadian and planetary biophysical environment, not a subsystem of the economy. The challenge is enormous, but we have no choice, both in terms of our own long-term survival and the survival of other species on whom we are dependent and with whom we share this planet.

Principles for a strategy of sustainability at the environmental, economic, and social levels have already been outlined in general terms, but some specific recommendations for Canada might be in order (see Standing Committee on Environment 1993):

**Environmental Sustainability** — The long-term viability of Canadian social, economic, and political institutions depends ultimately on the long-term sustainability of our biophysical resources. Governments should adopt new systems of national economic–ecological accounts to monitor the biosphere. The new indicators might include adjusted national product (ANP), consisting of GNP with the deduction of social and environmental costs. Other accounts would be set up to monitor, on an ongoing basis, the state of biological systems in terms of soils maintenance, pollution absorption, atmospheric regulation, and primary production (photosynthesis) (Rees 1990b). For example, Canadians have been liquidating their forests without knowing the full range of species and genetic diversity that exists and what is needed to ensure the ability of forests to maintain themselves over a long time. Similarly, the North Atlantic cod stocks may have reached the point of nonsustainability.

The Standing Committee on Environment (1993, p. 24) has recommended that, to meet our obligations under the Biodiversity Convention, we develop a National Biodiversity Strategy, part of which will be a national inventory of Canada's biological diversity. This will be undertaken by the federal government, but should be done in coordination with provincial and territorial governments. The United Nations Environment Programme (UNEP) should be expanded and budgeted to act as a principal source of environmental data, assessment, and reporting at the international level, as well as being able to monitor the critical changes needed by nation-states.

There is also a critical need to protect species and biodiversity, habitats, and ecosystems. Of prime importance here is the preservation of all representative ecozones and representative areas. Although both the Convention and the Green Plan call for increasing the protected land in Canada to 12 percent of the total land area from its current 3 or 4 percent, this still may be too low. In turn, there is a need to protect as many ecosystems as possible by the year 2000, as little is known about the sizes and types of areas needed for the long-term survival of many species.

Currently, about two-thirds of the 177 different ecoregions identified by Environment Canada have some form of representative area protection. Unfortunately, many of these areas may be too small to prevent the loss of biodiversity. Consequently, we should embark on a national course of action that will protect biological diversity not only in parks, ecological reserves, and other protected spaces but also in managed areas and the other 88 percent of Canada (Standing Committee on Environment 1993, p. 27). There must be a shift from industrial forestry and agriculture toward those forms of "ecoforestry" and "organic" agricultural practices that are better able to maintain a wide range of biological diversity and species.

Both the federal and provincial governments need to develop sustainability indicators that can monitor levels of environmental health. There must be clear and enforceable environmental standards, integrated both federally and provincially. This universality will become increasingly important in any movement toward greater devolution of the decision-making process at the community and regional levels.

**Economic Sustainability** — One of the most environmentally detrimental aspects of our current economic system is that we do not take account of its effects on natural ecosystems. Rarely do market prices factor in social costs or the costs to the environment of given products or manufacturing processes. In the short term, Canada must move quickly toward a form of full-cost accounting that factors into the price of a product its cost in human and environmental terms.

For example, it may be argued that the reason MacMillan Bloedel forest products can be sold so cheaply on the American market is because they do not have to factor in the immediate and long-term costs to the environment of clear-cutting. Nor does the processing of these products include the social costs resulting from ongoing labour-reducing technologies and lost opportunities in alternative economic and social options to this and future generations. Indeed, if such factors were integrated into the price of products, those forest goods derived from more environmentally benign forms of "ecoforestry" would be considerably cheaper. In this way, the market could be used to encourage the movement toward more sustainable forms of commerce. Similar full-cost accounting principles must also be used for agricultural and other products.

Canadians have been living far beyond their economic and environmental means. We have become a wealthy country because we have been recklessly converting natural environmental capital into financial capital. Moreover, we have been appropriating ecological capital from all over the world — and especially from the South — at a great cost to others in environmental and social terms. To achieve a sustainable society and economy, Canadians must drastically reduce their level of resource and energy consumption.

In terms of global equity, Southern societies will argue that Canada and other Northern nations should reduce their overall energy and resource usage by some 80 percent to be in keeping with their current 20 percent of the total global population. This would mean producing goods and products that last twice as long with half the current energy and resources. Federal and provincial governments should provide incentives and initial capital to encourage research into technologies and environmentally friendly forms of manufacturing. Environmental pollution and waste must be accounted for in highly efficient methods of production that take a "cradle to grave" approach to resource usage.

Canadians, now facing massive federal and provincial debts, must develop as much self-sufficiency as possible through economic diversification and by relying increasingly on the use of renewable resources. In turn, Canadian governments must be willing to link all trade agreements with foreign countries to high social and environmental standards.

**Social Sustainability** — Canada cannot move toward sustainability without addressing the employment crisis and its dual economic and social consequences. Governments working with the private sector must find ways to create opportunities for meaningful, sustainable employment with beneficial effects on economic, social, and bio-physical systems. We need ways to restore damaged ecosystems and derive a range of diverse products and value-added goods through the protection and sensitive use of such ecosystems as Canada's forests. We should also seriously consider methods of job sharing and a reduced work week, opening up the labour force to others in ways that still maintain human consumptive needs and, potentially, a higher quality of life for Canadian society as a whole.

For too long, environmental protection has been regarded as a hinderance to economic well-being. The opposite has usually proven to be true. Industries trying to avoid the high costs of waste disposal have often restructured their manufacturing processes and thereby become more efficient with substantial cost savings (Myer 1992, p. 42).

Canada must link its own sustainability strategy to an international strategy. We must set out to meet the Agenda 21 target of 0.7 percent of GNP for official development assistance (ODA) by no later than the year 2000. In turn, Canada must be willing to share in the transfer of information and technologies that can help other countries, both in the North and the South, to achieve their own forms of sustainability.

Canada should commit itself to reformulating national and international security policies. This should be done while recognizing that mutual global security should be predicated on global disarmament as well as on strategies for the South's economic sustainability and environmental protection.

The Canadian Constitution should be amended to include the following:

✦ A preambular provision recognizing the primacy of the Canadian environment and the obligation of all generations to preserve and enhance it, coupled with a related recognition that the Canadian environment is an integral, interdependent part of the global environment;

✦ Provisions from the Universal Charter of Environmental Rights; and

✦  Provisions from the International Covenant on Economic, Social, and Cultural Rights to augment Canada's Charter of Rights and Freedoms.

We need to get our priorities straight. The geosphere and the biosphere existed for billions of years before our species made its appearance, and the planet can exist without us. However, the converse is not true. To continue to survive, Canadians — along with the other members of the human global family — have no alternative but to adapt their behaviour and institutions to the imperatives of environmental stewardship and sustainability.

Here we may agree with the Brundtland Report in perhaps its most crucial conclusion. It will be excruciatingly difficult to make the required shift to save the planet's environment and also move toward parity between South and North. All such efforts must involve an unprecedented amount of "political will."

Do we have it?

# Bibliography

Bailey, S. 1990. Creating sustainable communities. Faculty of Graduate Studies, School of Community and Regional Planning, University of British Columbia, Vancouver, BC, Canada. Master's thesis.

Berlin, I. 1982. Against the current: essays in the history of ideas. Penguin Books, Harmondsworth, UK.

Bidwell, O. 1986. Where do we stand on sustainable agriculture? Journal of Soil and Water Conservation, 41(5), 317–319.

Bookchin, M. 1980. Toward an ecological society. Black Rose Books, Montreal, PQ, Canada.

Bouchard, L. 1990. Introduction. *In* A framework for discussion on the environment. The green plan. Environment Canada, Ottawa, ON, Canada.

British Columbia, Government of. 1992. A Land Use Charter: report on a land use strategy for British Columbia. Commission on Resources and Environment, Government of British Columbia, Victoria, BC, Canada. pp. 14–18.

British Columbia Round Table on the Environment and Economy. 1991. Sustainable communities. British Columbia Round Table on the Environment and Economy, Victoria, BC, Canada.

Brown, L.R. 1987. Sustaining world agriculture. *In* Brown, L.R.; et al., ed., State of the world. W.W. Norton, New York, NY, USA.

Bulkley Valley. 1992. Bulkley Valley Community Resources Board Agreement. Draft of October 11, 1991. Forest Planning Canada, 8(1), 7–10.

Burton, T.L. 1977. Natural resource policy in Canada: issues and perspectives. McClelland and Stewart Ltd, Toronto, ON, Canada.

Canada, Government of. 1991. Agriculture. The state of Canada's environment. Minister of Supply and Services, Ottawa, ON, Canada.

Canadian Council of Resource and Environment Ministers. 1987. Report of the National Task Force on Environment and Economy. Canadian Council of Resource and Environment Ministers, Downsview, ON, Canada.

Capra, F. 1986. Paradigms and paradigm shifts. Revision, 9(1), 11.

Cassirer, E. 1951. The philosophy of the Enlightenment. Princeton University Press, Princeton, NJ, USA.

Census Canada. 1992. Census overview of Canadian agriculture: 1971–1991. Ministry of Supply and Services, Hull, PQ, Canada. Catalogue 93-348.

Chiras, D.D. 1994. Environmental science: action for a sustainable future. Benjamin/Cummings Publishing Co., Redwood City, CA, USA.

Cholette, K. 1992. Tin Wis: an ecological project. The New Catalyst, 21 (Fall/Winter), 12.

Clow, M.J.L. 1990. Sustainable development won't be enough. Policy Options, 11(9), 6–8.

Corry, J.A. 1981. My life and work: a happy partnership. Queen's University Press, Kingston, ON, Canada.

Cotgrove, S.; Duff, A. 1980. Environmentalism, middle-class radicalism and politics. The Sociological Review, 28(2), 333–351.

Dalby, S. 1992. Security, modernity, ecology: the dilemmas of post-cold war security discourse. Alternatives: Social Transformation and Humane Governance, 17(1), 95–135.

Darling, C.R. 1991. In search of consensus: an evaluation of the Clayoquot Sound Sustainable Development Task Force process. University of Victoria Institute for Dispute Resolution, University of Victoria, Victoria, BC, Canada.

DeFries, R.S.; Malone, T.F. 1989. Global change and our common future. Papers from a forum. National Academy Press, Washington, DC, USA.

Devall, B.; Sessions, G. 1985. Deep ecology: living as if nature mattered. Peregrine Books, Salt Lake City, UT, USA.

Dover, M.; Talbot, L. 1987. To feed the earth: agro-ecology for sustainable development. World Resources Institute, New York, NY, USA.

Drengson, A. 1986. Ecological agriculture. In Magnusson, W.; Doyle, C.; Walker, R.B.J.; De Marco, J., ed., After Bennett: a new politics for British Columbia. New Star Books, Vancouver, BC, Canada.

Dunster, J. 1989. Concepts underlying a community forest. Forest Planning Canada, 5(6), 5–13.

Ecoforestry Institute. 1993. The Ecoforestry Institute. Ecoforestry Institute, Victoria, BC, Canada. Newsletter.

Edwards, C. 1990. The importance of integration in sustainable agricultural systems. In Edwards, C.A.; Lal, R.; Madden, P.; Miller, R.; House, G., ed., Sustainable agricultural systems. Soil and Water Conservation Society, Ankeny, IA, USA.

Emery, C. 1991. Share groups in British Columbia. Political and Social Affairs Division, Research Branch, Library of Parliament, Ottawa, ON, Canada.

Environment Canada. 1986. Wetlands in Canada: a valuable resource. Lands Directorate, Prime Wetlands Project, Ottawa, ON, Canada.

_____ 1987. Environment and development: a Canadian perspective. Minister of Supply and Services, Ottawa, ON, Canada.

_____ 1992. State of the environment report. Minister of Supply and Services, Ottawa, ON, Canada.

Evernden, N. 1985. The natural alien: humankind and environment. University of Toronto Press, Toronto, ON, Canada.

Forestry Canada. 1990. Forestry facts. Minister of Supply and Services, Ottawa, ON, Canada.

Fox, M. 1988. The coming of the cosmic Christ: the healing of Mother Earth and the birth of a global renaissance. Harper and Row, San Francisco, CA, USA.

Gardner, J.; Roseland, M. 1989. Acting locally: community strategies for equitable sustainable development. University of Waterloo, Waterloo, ON, Canada. Alternatives: Perspectives on Society, Technology and Environment, 16(3), 26–35.

Gayton, D. 1990. The wheatgrass mechanism: science and imagination in the western Canadian landscape. Fifth House Publishers, Saskatoon, SK, Canada.

Gever, J.; Kaufman, R.; Stole, D.; Vorosmarty, C. 1989. Beyond oil. In Daly, H.E.; Cobb, J.B., Jr., ed., For the common good: redirecting the economy toward community, the environment, and a sustainable future. Beacon Press, Boston, MA, USA.

Goldsmith, E. 1988. Gaia: some implications of theoretical ecology. The Ecologist, 18(2/3), 64–74.

Grant, G. 1980. Lament for a nation: the defeat of Canadian nationalism. Carleton University Press, Ottawa, ON, Canada.

Hall, J.; Hanson, A. 1992. A new kind of sharing: why we can't ignore global environmental change. International Development Research Centre, Ottawa, ON, Canada.

Hammond, H. 1991. Seeing the forest among the trees: the case for wholistic forest use. Polestar Book Publishers, Vancouver, BC, Canada.

Hardin, G. 1977. The tragedy of the commons. In Hardin, G.; Baden, J., ed., Managing the commons. W.H. Freeman and Co., San Francisco, CA, USA.

Head, I.L. 1991. On a hinge of history: the mutual vulnerability of South and North. University of Toronto Press, Toronto, ON, Canada.

Hopwood, D. 1992. Wise to give communities more influence in managing the public forests. Forest Planning Canada, 8(2), 20–21.

Howlett, M. 1990. The round table experience: representation and legitimacy in Canadian environmental policy making. Queen's Quarterly, 97(4), 580–601.

Laszlo, E. 1987. Evolution: the grand synthesis. New Science Library, Boston, MA, USA.

Lay, G.; Phillips, B. 1988. Community forest management: a discussion paper. Paper presented at the Conference on the Future Forest: Developing a Vision for Tomorrow, 4–6 March 1988, University of Victoria, Victoria, BC, Canada.

Loomis, R. 1990. Wildwood: a forest for the future. Reflections Publishers, Gabiola, BC, Canada.

Lovelock, J. 1988. The ages of gaia: a biography of our living Earth. W.W. Norton, New York, NY, USA.

Mabbutt, R. 1985. Managing community carrying capacity and quality of life: the Boise future foundation approach. Paper presented at the Symposium of New Perspectives on Planning in the West, March 1985, Arizona State University, Tempe, AZ, USA.

MacNeill, J. 1990. Sustainable development, economics and the growth imperative. The economics of sustainable development. Smithsonian Institution, Washington, DC, USA.

Mahood, C. 1991. Farmer's weapon is law of the land. Globe and Mail, 26 October 1991, pp. A1, A6.

Maslow, A. 1968. Toward a psychology of being. Van Nostrand, New York, NY, USA.

M'Gonigle, R.M. 1986. From the ground up: lessons from the Stein River Valley. In Magnusson, W.; Doyle, C.; Walker, R.B.J.; De Marco, J., ed., After Bennett: a new politics for British Columbia. New Star Books, Vancouver, BC, Canada.

_____ 1987. Local economies solve global problems. The New Catalyst, 7 (Spring), 4–5.

Milbrath, L. 1989. Envisioning a sustainable society: learning our way out. State University of New York, Albany, NY, USA.

Miller, G.T., Jr. 1988. Living in the environment. Wadsworth Publishing Co., Belmont, CA, USA.

Myer, S. 1992. Environmentalism and economic prosperity: testing the environmental impact hypothesis. Project on environmental politics and policy. Massachusetts Institute of Technology, Cambridge, MA, USA.

Nikiforuk, A. 1988. Harvest of despair. Report on Business, 1988 (June), 36–47.

Ophuls, W. 1977. Ecology and the politics of scarcity. W.H. Freeman and Co., New York, NY, USA.

Parr, J.F.; Papendick, R.I.; Youngberg, I.G.; Meyer, R.E. 1990. Sustainable agriculture in the United States. In Edwards, C.A.; Lal, R.; Madden, P.; Miller, R.; House, G., ed., Sustainable agricultural systems. Soil and Water Conservation Society, Ankeny, IA, USA.

Pearse, D.; Markandya, A.; Barbier, E. 1989. Blueprint for a green economy. Earthscan Publications Ltd, London, UK.

Penner, T.E. 1988. Hard times, hard choices: the prairie grain economy in transition. Western perspectives. Canada West Foundation, Calgary, AB, Canada.

Prigogine, I.; Stengers, I. 1984. Order out of chaos: man's new dialogue with nature. Bantam Books, Toronto, ON, Canada.

Prince, M. 1992. Sustainable development: its meaning and implications for Canadian social policy. Paper presented at the Conference on the Path to Brazil '92: Global Issues and the Environment, 21 February 1992, Victoria, BC, Canada. University of Victoria, Victoria, BC, Canada.

Raphael, R. 1981. Tree talk: the people and politics of timber. Island Press, Covelo, CA, USA.

Rees, W. 1988. Sustainable development: economic myths and ecological realities. The Trumpeter: Journal of Ecosophy, 5(4), 133–138.

_____ 1990a. Sustainable development and the biosphere: concepts and principles. Anima Books, Chambersburg, PA, USA. Teilhard Studies No. 23.

_____ 1990b. The ecology of sustainable development. The Ecologist, 20(1), 18–23.

_____ 1992. Video interview. *In* Ecology and development. Canadian ecology series. Open Learning Agency, Burnaby, BC, Canada.

Reganold, J.; Papendick, R.I.; Parr, J.F. 1990. Sustainable agriculture. Scientific American, 262(6), 112–120.

Robinson, P. 1986. Searching for alternative solutions: sustainable agriculture. Agriculture Canada, Winnipeg, MB, Canada. Policy Branch Working Paper.

Robinson, J.; Francis, G.; Legge, R.; Lerner, S. 1990. Defining a sustainable society: values, principles and definitions. University of Waterloo, Waterloo, Ontario. Alternatives: Perspectives on Society, Technology, and Environment, 17(2), 36–46.

Roche, D. 1993. A bargain for humanity: global security by 2000. University of Alberta Press, Edmonton, AB, Canada.

Rusk, J.; Vincent, I. 1992. Summit brought down to earth. Globe and Mail, 15 June 1992, pp. A1, A2, A10.

Salleh, A.K. 1984. Deeper than deep ecology: the eco-feminist connection. Environmental Ethics, 6(4), 339–345.

Science Council of Canada. 1992. Sustainable agriculture: the research challenge. Science Council of Canada, Ottawa, ON, Canada. Report No. 43.

Senate Standing Committee on Agriculture, Fisheries, and Forestry. 1984. Soil at risk: Canada's eroding future. Ministry of Supply and Services, Hull, PQ, Canada.

116 ◆ OFF COURSE

Shiva, V. 1989. Staying alive: women, ecology and development. Zed Books Ltd, London, UK.

Standing Committee on Environment. 1993. A global partnership: Canada and the conventions of the United Nations Conference on Environment and Development. Report of the Standing Committee on Environment. Government of Canada, Ottawa, ON, Canada.

Stinner, B.; Blair, J. 1990. Ecological and agronomic characteristics of innovative cropping systems. In Edwards, C.A.; Lal, R.; Madden, P.; Miller, R.; House, G., ed., Sustainable agricultural systems. Soil and Water Conservation Society, Ankeny, IA, USA.

Strong, M.F. 1992. Opening Address to the United Nations Conference on Environment and Development, 3–14 June 1992, Rio de Janeiro, Brazil. United Nations, New York, NY, USA.

Taylor, C., ed. 1982. Radical Tories: the conservative tradition in Canada. Anansi Press, Toronto, ON, Canada.

_____ 1977. The politics of the steady state. In Rotstein, A., ed., Beyond industrial growth. University of Toronto Press, Toronto, ON, Canada.

_____ 1992. Multiculturalism and the politics of recognition. Princeton University Press, Princeton, NJ, USA.

Taylor, D.M. 1990. Nature as a reflection of self and society. The Trumpeter: Journal of Ecosophy, 7(4), 174–176.

Taylor, J. 1926. Robert Burns: patriot and internationalist. Vancouver Burns Statue Fund, Vancouver, BC, Canada.

Thrupp, L. 1989. Politics of the sustainable development crusade: from elite protectionism to social justice in Third World resource issues. Energy and Resources Group, University of California, Berkeley, CA, USA.

Tisdall, P. 1992. Approaches to sustainable agriculture: seven case studies. Science Council of Canada, Ottawa, ON, Canada.

Travers, O.R. 1990. Economic and social benefits from BC's forests. Notes for a presentation at the Transition to Tomorrow: Community Options Forestry Conference, February 1991, University of Victoria, Victoria, BC, Canada.

_____ 1992. History of logging and sustained yield in BC, 1911–1990. Forest Planning Canada, 8(1), 39–48.

Turner, F. 1987. Rediscovering America: John Muir in his time and ours. Sierra Club Books, San Francisco, CA, USA.

UNCED (United Nations Conference on Environment and Development). 1992. Rio Declaration on Environment and Development. Principle 2. United Nations, New York, NY, USA.

Ussery, J.G. 1988. Local development in British Columbia: a case for community forestry. Environmental Studies Program, University of Victoria, Victoria, BC, Canada. Mimeo.

Vitousek, P.; Ehrlich, P.; Erlich, A.; Matson, P. 1986. Human appropriation of the products of photosynthesis. BioScience, 36, 368–374.

Warren, C.L.; Kerr, A.; Turner, A.M. 1989. Urbanization of rural land in Canada, 1981–86. Conservation and Protection Branch, Environment Canada, Ottawa, ON, Canada. State of the Environment Fact Sheet No. 89-1.

WCED (World Commission on Environment and Development). 1987. Our common future. Oxford University Press, New York, NY, USA.

Weiskal, T. 1989. The ecological lessons of the past: an anthropology of environmental decline. The Ecologist, 19(3), 98–103.

Wilde, K.D. 1984. Ecological knowledge and the next agricultural revolution. Man–Environment Systems, 14(5/6), 179–191.

Winner, L. 1986. The whale and the reactor: a search for limits in an age of high technology. University of Chicago Press, Chicago, IL, USA.

World Bank. 1991. World population projections, 1989–90. Short- and long-term estimates, tables 4 and 6. Johns Hopkins University Press, Baltimore, MD, USA.

# Index

# The Tao of Pooh

MacMillan Bloedel 75, 107
MacNeill, J. 3, 8–9
Mahood, C. 32
Malaysia 4, 102
malnutrition 23
maldevelopment 17
Malone, T.F. 89
Manitoba, farm growth in size 34
markets 75, 76, 81
Marx, Karl 25
Maslow, A. 64
materialism, standard of life 66
matter
    in a sustainable society 39, 40
    in a "throwaway" and sustainable
        society 39
    sustainable agriculture 83
mechanistic science 47
mechanization, BC forest companies
    35, 36
Meech Lake, debate 90
Meister Eckhart, Christian mysticism
    of 46
methane, emissions 101–102
Mexico, free trade with 30
M'Gonigle, R.M. 73, 76
Milbrath, L. 25
militarism, and ecology 50
Miller, G.T. 39
minority groups 90, 91
modernity
    Americans and Canadians and
        94–95
    and social ecology 50
    and the socialist tradition 51
    rejection of basic tenet of 48
monocultures 30, 33, 36, 86
Montreal Protocol 69, 98
Morris, William, political decentralism
    and egalitarianism 50–51
Muir, John 48
Mulroney administration 68–69, 95,
    100
multiculturalism 95
mutual obligation, and organic
    society 95–96
mutual sustainability 5, 16–17
mutual vulnerability 5, 16–17
Myer, S. 109
mysticism, influence on the modern
    environmental movement 46

Naess, Arne 49, 65
National Biodiversity Strategy 106
National Task Force Report, federal
    government 98
native peoples 81, 90, 99
natural gas, decision to sell to United
    States 25
natural processes
    forest management 71
    sustainable agriculture and 82
    thermodynamic irreversibility of
        58
natural resources
    alternatives to undue exploitation
        of 60
    Canada's policies and practices
        toward 44, 105
    managing of, aim 77
    reinvest wealth in maintenance
        of 41
    wise scientific management of 27
natural systems 55
    loss of 44
    maintenance of 58–60
    organic perspective of 50
    recognition of 58
nature
    alternative environmental
        paradigm 52
    as intrinsically valuable 49, 78
    celebration of by romantics 47
    communion with, Thoreau and
        Emerson 47
    Counter-Enlightenment and
        Romantic tradition 78
    dominant social paradigm 52
    domination of 50, 97
    "interest" of 54
    recognition of in selective logging
        methods 72
    remoteness from 64
    respect intrinsic value of 59, 78
    sanctity of 48
    World Charter of 104
negotiation, consensus-based,
    Clayoquot Sound 79
neocolonialism 15
neoconservatism 27, 95, 96, 97, 98
net primary production (NPP) 13–14
New Zealand 35
Newfoundland, fishing industry 21